It's Never Too Early, But It Can Be Too Late!

IT'S NEVER TOO EARLY, BUT IT CAN BE TOO LATE

A SELF-HELP BOOK ON GETTING YOUR AFFAIRS IN ORDER

DR. GENE W. LARAMY

In memory of my mentor, Dr. Elisabeth Kübler-Ross

Two Harbors Press
Minneapolis, MN

Two Harbors Press
212 3rd Avenue North, Suite 290
Minneapolis, MN 55401
612.455.2293
www.TwoHarborsPress.com

ISBN - 978-1-935097-99-0
ISBN - 1-935097-99-7
LCCN - 2010924962

Cover Photo © 2009. All rights reserved - used with permission.
Cover Design by Wes Moore
Typeset by Nate Meyers

Printed in the United States of America

DEDICATION

I dedicate this book to three of the finest young men who have ever lived,

my sons, Dan, Ron, and Charles

And to my wife, Inez,

the love of my life for over sixty years of marriage,

And in memory of my mentor,

Dr. Elisabeth Kübler-Ross,

author of the book *On Death and Dying,*

whose teachings have guided my life for many years

and who has been the inspiration for the writing of this book.

TABLE OF CONTENTS

PREFACE

Our society of today venerates youth. We try everything to "stay" young. We try cosmetics, to the tune of billions of dollars a year. We try tanning booths, exercises, workouts, hair dye, youth clothing, wearing our hair long—anything to make us look, act, and stay young.

Why is this? I believe it is to deny getting older, because that insinuates incapacitation or death. We can't, or at least don't want to, dwell on anything that spells "old age." By doing this, of course, we tend not to keep our affairs in order, because this, too, insinuates the end of life.

Unfortunately, young people can also become incapacitated, and, yes, they do also die. However, they almost always do not have their affairs in order, so when they do become incapacitated, the courts take over.

I think of two notorious cases that made headline news in papers and were prominent on TV news and in magazines, books, and the court system: Karen Ann Quinlan and Terri Schiavo. Schiavo's case actually went as far as the president's desk. For every case such as these two, there are thousands of similar cases every day throughout the world. If those in question had thought ahead and had their affairs in order, the cases would not have been strung out over years, and more than likely much pain and suffering would have been avoided, both for the deceased and their families.

Karen Ann was twenty-one years old when she became unconscious after coming home from a party. She had consumed Valium, Darvon painkiller, and alcohol. After she collapsed and twice stopped breathing for fifteen minutes or more, the paramedics arrived and took her to the hospital, where she lapsed into a persistent vegetative state. After she was kept alive on a ventilator for several months without improvement, her parents requested the hospital discontinue active care and allow her to die. The hospital refused, and legal battles ensued. Finally the courts relented and ruled in her parents' favor.

After she was removed from active life support she continued to live in a coma for almost a decade, until her death from pneumonia.

Quinlan's case continues to raise important questions in moral theology, bioethics, euthanasia, legal guardianship, and civil rights. Her case has affected the practice of medicine and law around the world. Two significant outcomes of her case were the development of formal ethics committees in hospitals, nursing homes, and hospices, and, more important, I believe, the development of advance health care directives. Had she had such directives filled out at the time, she more than likely would have died much sooner.

Terri Schiavo, age forty-one, collapsed in her home, perhaps a result of bulimia, and experienced respiratory and cardiac arrest on February 25, 1990, resulting in extensive brain damage, a diagnosis of persistent vegetative state, and fifteen years of institutionalization.

Terri was found in the hallway of their home by her husband, who immediately made a 911 call. Firefighters and paramedics arrived in response to the call and found her face-down and unconscious. She was not breathing and had no pulse. They attempted to resuscitate her; she was defibrillated several times and was transported to the hospital. There she was intubated, ventilated, and eventually given a tracheotomy. The long period without oxygen led to profound brain damage.

Her case in court went on for seven years, with her being in a vegetative state, before her husband was successful in getting a court order to remove the feeding tubes and letting nature take its course. He was opposed by her parents, who argued that she was in fact conscious and was improving.

In all, the Schiavo case involved fourteen appeals and numerous motions, petitions, and hearings in the Florida courts; five suits in federal district court; Florida legislation struck down by the Supreme Court of Florida; a subpoena by a congressional committee to qualify Schiavo for witness protection; federal legislation; four denials of *certiorari* from the Supreme Court of the United States; and even legislation that was signed by President George W. Bush designed to keep Schiavo alive.

As in the Quinlan case, all of this could have been avoided if Terri had filled out advance health care directives and had her affairs in order. Fifteen years of suffering, court battles, huge expenses, and survivors' mental anguish would not have happened.

This is why it is so important for everyone eighteen years of age and older to have their affairs in order—including filling out advance directives. This is why I have written this book. I have seen too many cases, such as the two mentioned above, to not try to improve the situation. We all need to be prepared. We all need to put our affairs in order. And it must begin at a young age to cover all bases, and all possible circumstances.

CHAPTER ONE
OVERVIEW

In more than forty years in the parish ministry, with a doctorate degree in counseling and the responsibility of the care and concern for the members and friends of the churches I have served, I have heard many sad stories. But the things I have heard more than anything else are: "My husband/wife has Alzheimer's; is incapacitated; he/she cannot speak or write; has died; and he/she took care of all our affairs, including the house decisions, financial decisions, checkbook, driving, etc., and I haven't the foggiest idea how to do these things or even know where the records are kept. I do not know what banks we use, how much money we have, or anything. I am at a complete loss. Can you help me?"

As an example, Dave (not his real name) and his wife, Ruth (not her real name), were on a vacation trip to Florida. They were staying with friends when Dave got up in the morning and was shaving in the bathroom, where he had a massive heart attack and died. Ruth was at a complete loss. Their friends helped them as much as possible, but a few days later she had to return to her home town to take care of funeral arrangements. She didn't have a clue as to what to do. I, of course, could help her with the funeral, but I was not able to help her with many of the other things, including her finances, of which I knew next to nothing. One day she told me that she had a letter from the bank saying she was overdrawn. She said, "How can this be, I still have checks in my checkbook?" She thought that as long as she had checks in the checkbook, it meant that she still had money to cover them. Ruth was not a mentally challenged individual; in fact, she was very bright and very sharp. She just never had to balance a checkbook, because Dave always did that.

Most of us have seen or heard the words: "You probably should get your affairs in order." We hear those words in television shows, movies, and from doctors. But even though we probably think we should do that "someday," we procrastinate, and

1

it doesn't seem to get done. We also think getting affairs in order is something only senior citizens should be concerned about. But, you know what? Young people can also become incapacitated or die. After all these years as a parish minister, I have come to the conclusion that any person over eighteen years of age should get, and keep, his or her affairs in order, because one never knows what tomorrow might bring. After something happens, it is too late.

I must admit that I had put it off until I began to write this book, but you can be sure I have taken care of it now. I have just been fortunate that nothing has happened before this.

Now, if you are the type of person who changes windshield-wiper blades on your car when the sun is shining, you may not need to read this chapter, or this book, for that matter. If, however, you are like most of us who typically overlook preventive maintenance, you should read further and consider heeding my advice.

When an adult dies or is incapacitated beyond being able to function, that person's loved ones are left not only with the grief resulting from what has happened, but also with the often very difficult task of identifying and locating property, money, and important documents that must be accounted for and possibly transferred. Because of the circumstances, it will not be a pleasant task at its best, but the practical burden may be greatly relieved by a little planning and organization.

I urge you to take the time, right after reading the remainder of this book, to put your affairs in order. Do it now. Do not "put it on the back burner" and say to yourself that you will get to it soon, because it is all too easy to procrastinate, and it will never get done.

A simple system of file folders, computer discs, or computer programs, properly labeled and all in the same location will make it much easier for your loved ones or survivors who end up with the task to handle necessary administrative, business, and financial matters after your incapacitation or death. In each chapter where I suggest forms, I will display the forms at the end of the chapter. Use the following checklist as a guide in assembling the contents for your file folders, computer discs, etc.

- ❏ A will, if you have one
- ❏ Trust documents
- ❏ Advanced directives (living will, medical power of attorney, etc.)
- ❏ Life insurance policies
- ❏ A list of organizations to which you belong that provide life insurance (credit unions, auto clubs, etc.)
- ❏ Health and accident insurance information
- ❏ Marriage certificates
- ❏ Divorce decrees, if any
- ❏ Birth certificates or adoption papers for you and your children

❑ Military papers (including discharge and Veterans Administration documents)
❑ Social Security numbers and documents
❑ Deeds to real estate
❑ Real estate loan documents (mortgages, deeds of trusts, etc.), and a complete list of your investments and property, including whom to contact about each
❑ Evidence of all bank accounts
❑ A reference to the location of all safety deposit boxes you rent and keys to each
❑ Automobile titles and reference to their whereabouts
❑ Evidence of money owed to you, such as promissory notes
❑ Reference and documents pertaining to money you owe, including charge accounts and loan account numbers
❑ Copies of recent income tax returns
❑ Instructions regarding your funeral or burial, if you have special requests. I will suggest later that you write your own obituary.
❑ Other important documents and information

So, you see, there are many decisions to be made every day in life . . . even late in life.

There are financial decisions, which include:
  • Making bank account deposits and withdrawals
  • Buying/selling a home or other property
  • Paying bills; arranging financing
  • Maintaining your will, deeds, life insurance, and other legal papers
  • Dealing with Social Security, Medicare, and other benefit programs
There are personal decisions, which include:
  • Choosing where to live: alone, with relatives, nursing home, etc.
  • Socializing with the people or groups you choose
  • Arranging recreation, travel, transportation
  • Fulfilling spiritual or religious preferences
  • Making funeral plans or burial arrangements
There are health decisions, which include:
  • Choosing a physical or health care facility
  • Employing home care providers
  • Consenting to or refusing treatment
  • Obtaining or disclosing medical records
  • Deciding upon the course of treatment in case of terminal illness

The law says these are *your* decisions to make and not somebody else's. You have the right to make choices based upon your own values, beliefs, and wishes, even if others disagree with you. Courts have almost always followed the expressed wishes of competent adults, especially in health care. Therefore, it is important to state your desires—*in writing*—about health and financial decisions when you are capable of clearly expressing your wishes.

However, what happens if you are sick or disabled and can't make these decisions yourself? If decision-making tools have not been set up in advance, very few states have "family consent" laws permitting other family members to make certain kinds of health care decisions on your behalf. In most states, no one, not even your spouse, has an automatic legal right to make any kind of decision on your behalf. A court petition may need to be filed to obtain this authority. This is usually called **guardianship** or **conservatorship** and can be time consuming, costly, and restrictive for everyone involved.

On the other hand, where decision-making tools have been set up in advance, your wishes will play a major role in controlling *who* makes those decisions for you and *what* those decisions are. You might think of these planning tools as a way of insuring your personal autonomy, much as you would insure your life or your health.

As this is just an overview of what is to follow, I will just list these tools here and go further in depth of each in later chapters.

For financial matters, the legal tools you can use are:
- Durable power of attorney
- Trusts (in selected cases)

For health-related, personal-choice matters, the legal tools you can use are:
- Medical power of attorney
- Living will

"But," you say, "I have a will, and almost everything I own is jointly held with my spouse. Do I really need any of these other legal tools?" Let's give this some consideration:

• WILLS

A will is an important part of planning for the future, but it deals only with events after your death. The legal tools described here are separate from your will—they deal with possible lifetime events up to the point of death.

• JOINT OWNERSHIP

Owning property jointly, such as a joint bank account, is a common and simple way to enable someone else to have automatic access to your property. However, it should be used cautiously. Joint owners can use the property as their own, and you may have little control over what a joint owner does. Moreover, a joint ownership is not helpful in handling property matters that may require your signature—such as transferring a house, car, or investments. Joint ownership does not protect you nearly as well as a durable power of attorney.

• DURABLE POWER OF ATTORNEY

What is it? It is a document by which one person (the "principal") gives legal authority to another (called the "agent" or "attorney-in-fact") to act on behalf of the principal.

What is it good for? It provides a simple way to appoint an agent or agents you want to manage any part or all of your affairs: financial, personal, or both. You can include instructions, guidelines, or limitations as you wish.

Creating: Generally must be signed and notarized. A few states have additional requirements.

IMPORTANT: In most states, power of attorney is durable only if the document states that it shall continue in effect (or take effect) after the onset of incapacity.

Things to think about: Determining when the principal has become "incompetent" may be a difficult issue.

Caution: Even though your agent acts as a "fiduciary," there is no formal oversight of the agent. If there is no one you fully trust to act as your agent, don't use this tool.

Bankers, brokers, and others sometimes hesitate to recognize durable power of attorney, but most will. Check with them ahead of time.

• TRUST

What is it? An arrangement under which one person or institution called the *trustee* holds the title to property for the benefit of other persons called *beneficiaries*.

What is it good for? Especially useful for lifetime management of property where there is a substantial amount of property and professional management is desired.

Has a high level of acceptance in business and financial community.

In most cases a trust will omit the necessity for your property to go through probate.

Creating: There is no special language, but it needs to be carefully drafted. This should be done by a lawyer.

A trust created for the lifetime management of property is known as an *inter vivos,* or "living" trust. There are two types: revocable living trust and an irrevocable living trust. The first you can opt out of at any time, the second you cannot opt out.

Things to think about: Professional management trusts can be costly to set up and manage.

A trust can create problems for public benefit eligibility.

It can be set up as a "standby" to be used only in the case of incapacity.

Use of a trust may have important tax consequences.

- ## MEDICAL POWER OF ATTORNEY

    What is it? This is the same as a durable power of attorney but directed exclusively at health care concerns.

    What is it good for? It enables you to appoint another person to make any or all health care decisions for you and to spell out guidelines for those decisions if you become incapacitated.

    Helps relieve the potential stress and conflict of decision-making for your family, friends, and health care providers.

    Creating: Usually the same as for a durable power of attorney, but special statutory requirements exist in some states.

    Things to think about: Choosing your agent is your most important decision. Make sure he or she knows your wishes, values, and preferences.

    This is a fairly new variation of the durable power of attorney. Lack of familiarity may be a problem.

    Make sure your doctors understand and will respect your wishes. The document should be made part of your medical record.

- ## LIVING WILL

    What is it? A written declaration that allows you to state in advance your wishes regarding the use of life-prolonging medical care if you become terminally ill and unable to communicate.

    What is it good for? It helps to insure that your wishes are known and carried out.

    (It is different from a medical power of attorney in that a living will does not appoint an agent and applies only to terminal illness.)

    Creating: Most of the states have a statute with a suggested form to use and instructions to follow for creating. Witness requirements, and notarization in particular, vary and must be strictly followed to be effective.

    Things to think about: Because the living will applies only in narrowly and sometimes unclearly defined circumstances, it is best to have both a living will and a medical power of attorney.

    An important question to address is "Do you want food and fluids withheld?"

Make sure your doctors understand and will respect your wishes. The document should be made part of your medical record.

The question is often asked, "What are my chances of becoming disabled and needing these tools?" Of course no one can give a satisfactory answer, but if we define disability as the need for assistance with activities of daily living, it is estimated that eight million persons in the United States are disabled, and most of them are elderly. Of course the chances of disability increase dramatically with age.

Who can help me do this advanced planning?

A lawyer who is familiar with "lifetime planning" or "planning for incapacity" will be your best resource. This is especially true for the preparation of a durable power of attorney or a trust. Standardized forms for these legal tools will not be tailored enough to meet your specific needs.

For a living will, many states have statutory forms you can use, or you can obtain forms from most hospitals or from the state attorney general. A few states have statutory forms for medical power of attorney. I have included a form that was made out for me by an attorney. Some states, such as Arizona, also have a DNR (do not resuscitate) form for EMTs (emergency medical technicians), which to be valid must be made out on an orange sheet of paper. I will also give an example of a wallet card you may reproduce.

Form - A

GENERAL INFORMATION

Name:		Spouse:	
Address:			
City:		State:	Zip:

Home Phone:		Work:		Cell:
Email address:				Fax:

Vital Information

Location of Will:

Location of Living Will:

Location of Power of Attorney:

Location of Medical Power of Attorney:

Location of Safety Deposit Box:

Location of Key for Safety Deposit Box:

Location of Home Safe or Security Box:

Combination and/or Location of Key for Home Safe:

Contents of Bank Safety Deposit Box:

Contents of Home Safe:

Form - B

IMPORTANT ADVISORS	
Doctor:	Phone:
Doctor:	Phone:
Doctor:	Phone:
Doctor:	Phone:
Doctor:	Phone:
Accountant:	Phone:
Stockbroker:	Phone:
Banker:	Phone:
Banker:	Phone:
Clergyman:	Phone:
Life Insurance Agent:	Phone:
Auto/Home Ins. Agent:	Phone:
Other Ins. Agent:	Phone:
Partner:	Phone:
Landlord:	Phone:
Trustee(s):	Phone:
Executor:	Phone:
Other:	Phone:
Other:	Phone:
Other:	Phone:
Other:	Phone:
Other:	Phone:

Form - C

IMPORTANT INFORMATION	
Name:	DOB:
SSN:	Employer:
Address:	
Spouse:	DOB:
SSN:	Employer:

Children	
Name:	DOB:
Address:	
Name:	DOB:
Address:	
Name:	DOB:
Address:	
Name:	DOB:
Address:	
Name:	DOB:
Address:	
Name:	DOB:
Address:	
Name:	DOB:
Address:	
Name:	DOB:
Address:	
Name:	DOB:
Address:	
Name:	DOB:
Address:	

CHAPTER TWO
FINANCES

A good part of this chapter is paraphrased, with permission, from a book written by my good friends Don and Sue Larkin, *Enjoying the Riches of Retirement* (Danke Publishing, 1987). Don and Sue are both certified financial planners, who together have spent more than forty years informing retirees, and the soon to be retired, about the best ways to make this important part of every American's life more enjoyable and rewarding. I highly recommend this book as a help in getting your affairs in order.

To build a financial program with scope and direction, it is necessary, as it is in building a house, to start with a solid foundation. There are probably as many ways to do this as there are financial planners, but most financial planners will begin by recommending that a person have an up-to-date will.

Now if you think the preparation of a will is a gloomy task, putting it off indefinitely will in no way prolong your life. And if you do not indicate how you want your estate distributed (no matter how large or small it is), *the state will do it for you.* Each state has different laws governing who gets what when a person dies intestate (without a will), and one thing is certain: the law defining distribution of your assets is likely to be quite different from what you think it should be.

The cost of having a simple will prepared is quite inexpensive, compared to the anxiety and other problems that not having one can create for your loved ones. A competent professional can design a document that is specific to your financial needs and circumstances and can preclude future claims.

You can greatly assist your attorney by anticipating some needs and making some advanced decisions concerning your estate and your heirs. If you are married, you should discuss these matters with your spouse and make your plans together.

This is especially important for women, who generally outlive men and constitute 80 percent of all widowed people.

After your will is completed, it should be kept in a safe place, but one that is accessible by others after your death. It is not recommended that a will be placed in a bank safety deposit box, as some jurisdictions will require that the box be sealed immediately upon your death.

Consider leaving it with your attorney, a bank or trust company, or the individual that you have named as executor of your will. It is also a good idea to leave a memo with your family members describing its location, along with the location of your important papers, so that it can't be missed.

The job of creating a will is not complete in itself, however. A will must be periodically reviewed, to make sure you still wish it to remain as it is. Circumstances change over time. People get married, divorced, have children, and so on. The government is always looking for ways to confuse us with estate, gift, and inheritance taxes.

You can change your will either by writing a completely new document or by amending the present one with what is termed a "codicil." Certain legal restrictions and forms must be followed, however, and these may vary depending on your location.

Probate:

Probate is a word that comes from the Latin *probatum*, "a thing approved." Extending as far back as 1066, it is essentially the governmental approval that a will is authentic.

Probate was originally created to protect the last wishes of the deceased, but it can become a very expensive and time-consuming matter that may be out of step with our times and your needs and desires.

The will is, after all, the most contested of all legal documents. The questions that arise are: "How can you avoid probate?" and "Should you avoid probate?"

One of the most comprehensive and perceptive analyses of the probate system done to date is a two-year study by attorneys who were commissioned by the American Association of Retired Persons, entitled: *A Report on Probate: Consumer Perspectives and Concerns*, published in 1994.

This study produced some very convincing evidence that the probate process is inflicting undue strain and emotional and financial stress on the unsuspecting public. It also presented a strong message that consumers should be educated about the evils of probate and about simple alternatives to avoid it.

Sadly, after publishing this revealing study about probate practices, AARP did little to publicize the existence of this excellent document. Within months they put the study on the back shelf, after the will and probate attorneys began advertising in the AARP magazine declaring that probate was not all that bad. Thus, thousands of retired people—those needing the advice the most—failed to learn about the horrors and financial consequences of the tactics being used by some will and probate attorneys.

The AARP report found that often attorneys lay the groundwork for their probate practice by writing wills. Some use wills as a "loss leader." They write wills cheaply, as a way to generate other business—specifically, future probate business.

The AARP study noted that John McCabe, the legislative director for the National Conference of Commissioners on Uniform State Laws, once remarked, "The probate process has been a cash cow for attorneys. Small firms and solo practitioners in probate practice do far better than just pay the phone bills with these fees. They make a very good living on them."

The AARP study analyzed three states—California, Wisconsin, and Delaware—as the most representative of the three different methods nationwide of charging probate fees. The study found that the average time of probate process was two years and three months, and the average cost of probate (court) consumed *5 to 10 percent* of the gross estate. (Gross estate is the total value of your estate prior to any reductions for liabilities such as mortgages or loans), and the document stated that "in some cases, attorney fees consumed *20 percent* or more of estate value. This is especially true of small estates.

The AARP study convincingly affirms that probate is unnecessary! If the only function of probate is to pay creditors who aren't using the process in the first place, then probate is an obsolete system foisted on an unwilling public for the sole purpose of lining attorneys' pockets—and *$25 billion to $50 billion* annually in probate fees is a tempting gold mine for too many attorneys.

The AARP study found that a startling *90 percent* of all estates of widows and widowers age sixty and above will go through probate. Therefore, education is drastically needed.

The study also recommended that "state and local bar associations should require members of the probate bar, when drafting a will, to disclose the estimated costs of the eventual probate proceeding: *"Clients should be informed of any percentages currently charged for probate and how this might affect the assets they intend to pass to survivors."*

The AARP study made some very strong recommendations that consumers be educated about the evils of probate and about simple alternatives. Specifically, the study recommended that "aging organizations should provide more information to older consumers about estate planning issues, including *(1) information about the procedural and cost problems of probate . . . and (2) information about alternatives to probate such as living trusts."*

So, some of the problems with probate are very apparent. The average time can vary from ten months to two years, and once it is filed, all the records become public.

You don't have to have a lawyer, of course, but probate is more complicated than people think. The process is lengthy because all heirs and creditors must be notified by mail and in the newspaper. An inventory and appraisal must be made of everything you have. And several months must be given for creditors to file any claims. One of the things that is often misunderstood is that in probate your house, for instance, is listed at appraised value, not the equity amount.

Also, if you own property in another state, a second probate must be started. This can result in doubling attorney fees and other costs, which are usually based on the size of the estate.

While a will goes through probate, the court freezes assets in the estate until it approves the will, attorney fees and other costs must be paid out of the heirs' pockets.

To avoid probate, consider what goes through probate: property that you are considered to have owned at the time of your death. Whatever you don't legally own at the time of your death is not subject to probate.

Living Trust:

A great alternative to a will, which must go through probate, is the **revocable living trust,** which does not have to go through probate. What are the advantages of a revocable living trust?

1. Completely avoids probate fees.
2. Can reduce or eliminate estate taxes.
3. Keeps your estate private and confidential.
4. Estate can be settled in as little as 1–3 days.
5. You retain 100 percent control of all assets.
6. Prevents conservatorship in the event you become incompetent.
7. Eliminates emotional stress on your family.
8. Completely revocable, can be changed or canceled by you at any time.
9. Avoids contestability.
10. Easy to set up and maintain.

With this in mind, and if your estate warrants it, you may want to seriously look into a revocable living trust. Such a trust is settled without a court proceeding, it is private, and the assets are not frozen. Unlike a will, it can be changed without the need for a lawyer, and it is more difficult to contest.

Of interest, it is a *living* document and can make provisions for your needs in the event that you are temporarily incapacitated.

How does it work? Basically, the titles to all property—real estate, stocks, automobiles, bank accounts, whatever—are placed in a trust while you are alive. In other words, you do not own anything; the trust owns all your assets. A trust document serves the same purpose as a will and outlines instructions to a trustee on how you want the assets managed and distributed.

One of the beauties of a revocable living trust is that you can act as your own trustee, if you wish, so there is no loss of control and no management fees. And unlike with wills, both spouses can use the same trust, and one trust can hold property in any number of states.

About the only hassles involved are transferring the titles of all your property into the name of the trust. The initial cost is more than the price of a will, but it is considerably cheaper in the long run.

Other possibilities for avoiding probate include joint tenancy with right of survivorship or tenancy by the entireties—which are like joint tenancy but are strictly for spouses.

But, the question is asked, should you really avoid probate? Estates produce income that is subject to income tax during the time the estate is in probate. But because the probate estate is considered a new and separate taxpayer, you could get some beneficial tax savings.

In addition, probate forces creditors to put their claims on the table within a certain period of time. If they don't make those claims within that period, they are out of luck.

To make the necessary decisions, you should discuss with a good financial planner whether your estate is in that taxable bracket or not. Ask about the advantages of trusts as they apply to you. Perhaps it would be more advantageous to consider annual small gifts, the irrevocable transfers of life insurance policies, or other options that may apply.

And, of course, discuss the most important matter: what is best for your family?

Once the question of probate or living trusts has been handled, it is time to move up to the next part of your financial foundation—the emergency fund.

An emergency fund is a crucial part of getting your affairs in order and deserves thorough consideration. The purpose of such a fund is to cover expenses not planned for or covered by insurance, so that they can be taken care of without affecting your standard of living.

Such expenses could include such things as an unexpected trip to visit or care for a relative, attendance at a funeral out of state, major appliance or auto repair, financial assistance for your children or grandchildren, medical expenses, a terrific travel opportunity, or simply a safety cushion for peace of mind.

Because it is an *emergency* fund, the dollars in it should be readily available and liquid. This should be between 10 and 15 percent of whatever money you have available for investment purposes. If you are not yet retired, an equivalent amount would be between three and six months' income.

This money should be invested strictly in *guaranteed* accounts with liquidity. Guaranteed accounts will give you the lowest yield, but they are also the safest, and your emergency money needs to be safe.

There are, of course, many other financial matters to cover that are far beyond my expertise, so the best thing to do is contact a reputable financial planner as soon as possible to get your affairs in order; then you can truly have peace of mind. Remember, at any age you may need your affairs in order.

Form - D

DOCUMENT LOCATIONS / BANK INFORMATION

CATEGORY	ITEM DESCRIPTION	LOCATION
WILLS	Original Will of Husband	
	Original Will of Wife	
	Estate Planning Letter	
TRUSTS	Revocable Living Trust	
BUSINESS PAPERS	Inventory of Business Interest	
	Assets	
	Partnership Agreements	
	Corporation Documents	
	Other	
	Other	
SECURITIES	Inventory of Stocks	
	Inventory of Mutual Funds	
	Inventory of Bonds	
BANK ACCOUNTS		

Form - E

BANK ACCOUNTS		
BANK NAME	CHECKING #	SAVINGS #

CREDIT CARD INFORMATION	
ACCOUNT NUMBER	OUTSTANDING BALANCE

Form - F

OUTSTANDING LOANS	ACCOUNT #	INSTITUTION	BALANCE
Mortgage			
Mortgage			
Automobile			
Automobile			
Life Insurance Policy			
Life Insurance Policy			

LIFE INSURANCE COMPANY	POLICY #	FACE AMOUNT	LOANS AGAINST POLICY

OUTSTANDING DEBTS TO BE COLLECTED		
Name	Address	Balance

CHAPTER THREE
ADVANCE DIRECTIVES

As I am sure most of you know, there was considerable confusion, on both sides of the issue, at the time of Terri Schiavo's dying and death. If only she had made out advance directives forms telling her family, doctors, clergyperson, or whoever concerned, what she would like to have happen in the event of her inability to speak for herself, all this confusion and turmoil would not have taken place. And, remember, she was a very young lady.

When I was an associate minister of a church in Sun City, Arizona, during the 1980s and '90s, one of my duties was to line up speakers for a brown-bag luncheon program that met once a week. One of the speakers I lined up was a lawyer (who later became a very good friend) who talked on the subjects of wills, living wills, and medical power of attorney. My wife and I were so impressed by his presentation that we made an appointment right then to have him help us make out our wills as well as our advance directives. I will include in this chapter the forms with which he helped us, as well as information about every state in the United States regarding living wills, medical power of attorney, and organ donation. I found that most states will honor these forms, but to be on the safe side you should always ask an attorney, or a responsible official from the state government in the state in which you live, as to these forms' validity in your state. If you spend time in two or more states, you should also be aware of the laws in each of the states regarding advance directives, as these laws may differ. Likewise, if you move from one state to another, make sure that your advance directives pass muster in the new state.

Because our constitutional rights to privacy and liberty generally are interpreted to include the right to make our own medical treatment decisions, all states now have laws that allow us to make future health decisions so that if we become incapacitated and unable to make such decisions later on, our family and doctors will know what medical care we want or do not want. State laws allow us to appoint a person to make future health care treatment decisions for us if we become incapacitated, since we cannot predict what future decisions might be necessary. You should give careful thought as to who that person might be.

Because the laws differ somewhat from state to state, the federal Medicare and Medicaid agency suggests that citizens contact their state's attorney general's office about the laws of that state.

The government also has interests in some of our medical treatment decisions, which include preserving life, safeguarding the integrity of the medical profession, preventing suicide, and protecting innocent third parties (Arizona, for instance, does not approve or authorize assisted suicide).

In the state of Arizona, if a person becomes unable to understand reason or make judgments, his or her constitutional rights to make medical treatment decisions remain. A health care representative appointed by the person in writing, or, if no one has been appointed, a representative appointed according to law, will make treatment decisions as follows:

1. Be guided or controlled by medical treatment decisions that were made in writing by the person before he/she became incapacitated.
2. Using Substitute Judgment: The representative will make choices about treatment decisions based on what he/she believes the incapacitated person would choose. If these choices are unknown, then the representative will decide based on what he/she knows about the incapacitated person's values.
3. Using Good Faith to Decide Best Interests: If the representative does not know the decisions, preferences, or values of the incapacitated person as to medical treatment decisions, then he/she must decide in good faith what would be in the best interests of that person, considering (a) relief from suffering, (b) whether functioning will be preserved or restored, and (c) the quality and extent of sustained life.

Perhaps it would help to become familiar with some of the medical subjects that relate to future medical care, especially medical treatment choices specifically mentioned in Arizona law.

Comfort Care

Under Arizona law, comfort care is an effort to protect or enhance the quality of life without artificially prolonging it. Comfort care often means pain medication. For example, morphine and other narcotics may be administered to alleviate pain, and dosages can be increased as pain increases. Medications may or may not cause sleepiness, sedation, or other side effects.

Comfort care can also include oxygen, and perhaps stopping certain medical interventions. It may involve offering, but not forcing, food or fluids, keeping the patient clean, using ice chips and wet cloths, humidifying the room, turning lights on or off, holding the patient's hand and comforting him/her with soothing words and music.

Cardiopulmonary Resuscitation (CPR) and Artificial Breathing

CPR was developed to assist victims facing sudden death, such as heart attack or trauma, to increase the likelihood of long-term survival. Unless a doctor or other licensed health care provider authorizes a DNR (do not resuscitate) or have a valid pre-hospital medical care directive, CPR is administered virtually every time a person's heart stops.

Ventilators put air and therefore oxygen into the lungs and thus can save lives. Oxygen is administered for a short term by a tube through the nose or mouth and for a longer term by a tracheotomy (a hole in the throat).

Artificially Administered Foods and Fluids

Foods and fluids can be artificially administered by medically invasive procedures such as intravenous treatment or by various types of tubes inserted into the body. (If foods and fluids can be taken by spoon, drink, or other natural means, they are not considered artificially administered.)

Now that you are familiar with a few of the issues, you should consider the people with whom you can begin your life-care planning conversations. Your medical care is about you—so *you* should start the conversations with those who can help you consider what medical treatments you might want or not want if you become incapacitated, or as you approach the end of your life.

First of all, think about whom you might want as your representative to make decisions for you if you become unable to do so yourself. This should be a person you trust to have your interests at heart—someone who can make decisions for you in a manner that is consistent with your preferences, *even* if he or she disagrees.

Be sure that you speak with your representative about your choices, so that he or she can make medical decisions on your behalf in the way you would want. Remember, your representative may be asked to make many medical decisions for you if you become incompetent or cannot communicate your wishes—not only ultimate life-and-death, turn-off-the-machine decisions, but also decisions about day-to-day medical care, placement in a nursing home, hospital, or hospice care, or administration of certain medication. As the old saying goes, "Watch how you treat your children, as they will be the ones who will no doubt choose your nursing home."

Consider sharing your thoughts about some or all of the above issues with your spouse and children and whoever is closest to you, as they are the most likely to be affected emotionally, or in other ways, by your medical condition and the decisions that must be made. Sometimes problems arise because family members do not understand what the patient would want in a given situation, or they disagree about what treatment is best for the patient. Although the designated representative is legally empowered to make decisions on behalf of the patient, uncertainties can cause concern to the treating physicians and can result in problems, delays, misunderstanding, and even court proceedings.

This is why it is so important that you discuss your beliefs, values, and preferences about medical care not only with the person you choose as your health care representative, but also with family, relatives, and close friends whom you have not chosen to represent you if you become incompetent. This will give them an opportunity to learn from you what medical care you want and will make decisions easier for your representative and your physicians, should the time come when you cannot make medical decisions for yourself.

You can get medical information about many issues related to life-care planning forms, but only your doctor can give you the personal medical advice you need to make the best choices for you. Do not hesitate to talk with your doctor about these forms and ask his or her opinion about what is best for you.

You may very well have religious beliefs that influence your choices. Discuss your choices with your clergyperson. You can also learn more about the positions of different faiths from religious magazines, newspapers, or Internet web pages published by various faith groups.

Finally, a lawyer, accountant, banker, or others with whom you have a relationship may also have advice about life-care planning and choices that are best for you.

Ultimately, however, it is up to you to make the final decisions.

I personally believe that a person should consider his or her values, beliefs, and preferences as to the length of his or her life in relation to the quality of life, and whether he or she would, or would not, choose to prolong that life regardless of the quality.

Ask yourself the following questions:
- What does quality of life mean to me?
- Which of the following, or other factors, are important to me in considering the quality of my life? The ability to think for myself? Consciousness? The ability to communicate? The ability to take care of my personal needs? My privacy and dignity? Mobility? Independence and self-sufficiency? The ability to recognize family and friends?
- What are my responsibilities?
- Are there people I feel I have an obligation to live for? Who? Are there duties I feel I have an obligation to live for? What duties?

- Do my choices change if my obligations to those persons or duties are resolved?
- Does my age play a factor in any or all of my choices? Do my preferences change depending on how old I might be if and when these decisions must be made?
- What is the importance of my religious beliefs or other values in making these determinations? Whom can I talk to about this?
- Is my future living environment an important consideration for me?
- How do I feel about living in a nursing facility or other medical care facility for ongoing medical treatment?
- Is financial cost a consideration for me when I think about disability or end-of-life matters?
- What aspects of finances should I consider?
- Under what circumstances do I want some, all, or no life supports to be administered? To be withheld? To be removed or stopped? Why? Which?
- What about withholding or withdrawing life-sustaining treatment if I am known to be pregnant and there is the possibility that with treatment the embryo or fetus will develop to the point of a live birth?
- What about medical care necessary to treat my condition until my doctors reasonably conclude that my condition is terminal or is irreversible and incurable or I am in a persistent vegetative state?

Other questions to ponder and decide upon: What do you want done as far as organ donation? You can determine if you want to donate organs or tissues, and if you do then what organs or tissues do you want to donate: Heart? Liver? Lungs? Kidneys? Pancreas? Intestine? Cornea? Bones? Skin? Heart valves? Tendons? Ligaments? Some or all of the above? For what purposes, and to what organizations? Or you can leave the choice to your representative.

Do you have preferences about what tissues or organs to donate? Do you have preferences as to what uses might be made under the laws of your state for your tissues or organs: Transplantation? Therapy? Medical or dental education? Research or advancement of medical or dental science? Some or all of these uses?

Still another decision: Under Arizona law, an autopsy may be required when a person dies who was not under the current care of a physician for a potentially fatal illness, and/or the physician is unavailable or unwilling to sign a death certificate. This might happen if a person dies at home. However, if the person's doctor is willing to sign a death certificate, or if the person is under the care of a hospice and its physician will sign the death certificate, an autopsy will probably not be required.

If there is no legal reason to require an autopsy, you can decide whether upon your death you want an autopsy or not, or whether you want your representative to choose for you. There is usually a charge for a voluntary autopsy. After the autopsy is completed, the body is transported to the mortuary for burial or cremation. This can certainly be a sensitive topic at the time of death, and you can help your family and loved ones by making your preference clear.

Do you want comfort care and other support while you are dying? What are your preferences and directions about pain and pain medication? Do you want a comfort care medication or procedure even if it might make you drowsy, sedated, or has other effects? Do you want certain people to be with you when you are dying, if they can do so? If so, whom? Do you have preferences about where you want to die? At home? In a hospital? Hospice? Or somewhere else? Do you want your church, synagogue, or mosque advised if you are dying? Do you want certain music, poetry, or religious readings? Do you want silence? Radio? Television?

Remembrances to loved ones and funeral or other arrangements: Do you have anything you want to be remembered for, or any special words to share with anyone that you would like to write down? Do you want to be buried or cremated? Do you have preferences about a memorial service? What? Where? When? Do you want to write your own obituary? If you have a copy, where is it? Are there certain people you would like to attend your service? Act as pallbearers? Are there any favorite hymns, songs, Bible passages? Are there rituals you would like—military honors for example, or fraternal organization services?

Now, after answering all the above questions, it is time to look at the forms and fill them out. After they are filled out, you should keep the originals in a safe place, but also keep them handy, so you can review them from time to time and make sure you still agree with what you have stated. Give copies of the forms to all members of your family, and to close loved ones. Also, give a copy to your representative(s), your doctor(s), and the hospital where you will likely receive care. Keep a few extra copies, and be sure to take one with you if you go to the hospital or other health care facility, if that facility doesn't already have a copy on file.

Many states, of which Arizona is one, maintain an advance-directive registry, which is a confidential database that will store a copy of your completed advance health care directives. The purpose of registering these forms is to create a centralized location where your relatives, or the hospital or other health care facility caring for you, can access the form if it is not readily available. Access to the forms in the registry is password protected.

If you would like to register your forms in the Arizona Advance Directive Registry, you should contact the Office of the Arizona Secretary of State. Most other states will have the same type of arrangements.

You may change, correct, or cancel these forms whenever you wish. You should review the forms every year or so, to consider whether to make changes based on your life circumstances. You should initial and date the forms every time you look at them. Remember to discuss changes with your family, your representative, your doctors, your clergyperson, your hospital, or anyone else who needs to know.

If at any time you change your directives, you should complete a new form, following all the instructions. Be sure to put a date on the new form, since the most recent form will be the valid form. It is a good idea to gather the original form and copies of the old form and destroy them. Give a copy of the new form to your representative, your family members, your doctors, and any others you want to know about your wishes.

Even though all states have laws for advance health care directives or life-care planning, the laws may be somewhat different. Normally the law of the state where the treatment occurs controls, not the law of the state where medical forms were signed. If you spend time in more than one state and reasonably conclude you may need medical treatment in more than one state, you might want to have your forms comply with the laws of the states where you might be treated, to the extent possible. It would behoove you to consult an attorney for help with this.

Most people communicate their health care directives by completing forms such as a living will or a durable medical power of attorney. There are also other adjunct forms that we will be discussing.

Almost all states have forms that can be downloaded from the web, especially if you use the Google search engine, by entering "state name / advance directives" in the search box. Most will also have an article listing "procedures and the law" pertaining to advance directives in that particular state.

One thing that should be made very clear before you fill out any forms pertaining to advance directives: this procedure involves more than simply filling out forms. *The time you spend thinking about the kind of care you want, or don't want, and discussing your wishes with your family and loved ones is much more meaningful and important than simply checking off boxes on a form. The written documents are a good way to record your thoughts and desires, but it is no substitute for time spent discussing those choices with your loved ones.*

A case in point: though I served as a parish pastor for many years, I shall never forget one particular instance where a person had made out living-will forms and listed his desire for immediate cremation. Several members of his family went along with his desire, and he was cremated as scheduled. However, one daughter, who did not live in the area and with whom he had not discussed his wishes, came unglued psychologically because she simply could not accept that her father had been "burned up." This, of course, caused a great deal of confusion, stress, and hurt within the family—something they did not need in a time of sorrow. I had to counsel this person for over a year before she could accept what had happened. She nearly had a complete psychological breakdown over something that could very well have been avoided had her father discussed his wishes ahead of time. This is just one example of the many times I was forced to intercede in family disputes over advanced directives. Again, remember that when you make out your own living will, it is your loved ones, not you, who will have to live with your decisions. My advice is to make it as easy as possible on your loved ones, as they will already have more than enough with which to cope at the time of your death.

In my ministry I have been asked many times the differences between burial and cremation, and what the church has to say about cremation. My answer has always been that the results of burial and cremation are actually the same. With burial there is slow oxidation, and with cremation there is fast oxidation. As far as what the church has to say about it, you might want to consult your own clergyperson, but I have never found any place in the Bible that discusses it in any form, nor have the churches I have served favored one method over the other. I firmly believe it is up to the person and the person's family to do whatever they wish.

Filling out one's own "death wishes" is not easy. It is understandable that we should be reluctant to think of our own death. It has been said that it is impossible to look directly into the sun, and it is also impossible to look directly at our own death. Even as we look at, or think about, our own death, we are looking at it as an observer, not as the person who is dying. It is to save those who are dear to us as much suffering and anguish as is humanly possible, when the event of our death occurs, that we choose to make all possible arrangements ahead of time.

Such decisions made now not only contribute to our peace of mind, but are intended to relieve our loved ones, relatives, and friends of these responsibilities later, when they are under the stresses of grief and loss. Open discussion and thoughtful planning with our families should be both reassuring to us and of great assistance to those we leave behind.

One caution, however, as said before, don't have your final wishes "set in concrete." Remember, you do not have to live with the final decisions you make, but your loved ones do. All these arrangements are made to help them in planning and preparing for your demise. But they should have the final say in everything, other than the decisions that are made for your dying process. You alone must make those decisions.

Included in this book are brief descriptions of the alternatives, a statement (to be filled out) regarding what you would like done, and instructions as to where all records pertinent to the settlement of your estate may be found.

The following is a copy of the Living Will and Medical Power of Attorney made out for me by an attorney in the state of Arizona in 1995. These forms are probably much more detailed than the forms presently available, but they give you some things to think about.

LIVING WILL
of
GENE W. LARAMY

THIS DECLARATION Is made pursuant to section *36-3201 et seq. of the Arizona Revised Statutes.* For purposes of this declaration the terms "attending physician," "declaration," "life sustaining procedure" and "terminal condition" shall have the meanings ascribed to them by *Section 36-3201 of the Arizona Revised Statutes* and any successor provisions thereto.

I, _____, being of sound mind, willfully and voluntarily make known my desire that my dying not be artificially prolonged under the circumstances set forth below and declare that:

If at any time I should have an incurable injury, disease or illness certified to be a terminal condition by two (2) physicians who have personally examined me, one of whom is my attending physician, and the physicians have determined that my death will occur unless life-sustaining procedures are used, and if the application of life-sustaining procedures would serve only to artificially prolong the dying process, I direct that life-sustaining procedures be withheld or withdrawn and that I be permitted to die naturally with only the performance of medical procedures deemed necessary to provide me with comfort care.

I further direct that if at any time I should be in a permanent vegetative state or an irreversible coma as certified by two (2) physicians who have personally examined me, one of whom is my attending physician, and the physicians determine that the application of life-sustaining procedures, including artificially administered food and fluids, will only artificially prolong my life in a permanent vegetative state or irreversible coma, I direct that these procedures, including such artificial administration of food and fluids, be withheld or withdrawn and that I be permitted to die naturally with only the administration of medication to alleviate pain or the performance of other medical procedures necessary to provide me with comfort care.

I declare that if I am unable to give directions regarding the use of life-sustaining procedures, it is my desire that this Declaration be honored by my family and attending physician as the final expression of my legal right to refuse medical of surgical treatment, and I hereby accept the consequences of such refusal.

I declare that I understand fully the nature of this Declaration, and I have the emotional and mental capacity to make this Declaration.

IN WITNESS WHEREOF, I have hereunto set my hand this _____ day of _____, 1995

_____
(signature)

_____
(Printed Name)

S. S. Number:_____

WE, THE UNDERSIGNED, witnesses, herby sign our names to this instrument, and being first duly sworn, do hereby declare to the undersigned authority that the declarant signs and executes this instrument as *his* Living Will, that *he* signs it willingly, that *he* executes it as *his* free and voluntary act for the purposes therein expressed; and that each of us, at the request of the declarant and in the presence and hearing of the declarant, signs this Living Will as witness to the declarant's signing, and that to the best of our knowledge the declarant is over the age of majority, of sound mind and under no constraint or undue influence at the time of signing.

In addition, we the undersigned witnesses, further state that we are not: (1) related to the declarant by blood or marriage; (2) at the time of declaration, entitled to any portion of the estate of the declarant under a Will of the declarant or a codicil to a Will then existing or by operation of law then existing; (3) claimants against any portion of the estate of the declarant a the time of his decease or at the time of the execution of the declaration; and (4) directly financially responsible for the declarant's medical care.

_____
WITNESS

_____
WITNESS

STATE OF ARIZONA   )
) ss.
County of Maricopa   )

           SIGNED, SWORN TO AND ACKNOWLEDGED before me, the undersigned Notary Public, by _____, the declarant, and signed and sworn to before me by each of the above witnesses, on this ___ day of _____, 1995.

_____

NOTARY PUBLIC
My Commission Expires:

_____
(Date)

MEDICAL POWER OF ATTORNEY

KNOW ALL MEN BY THESE PRESENTS:

That, I, _____, a Principal, herby make, constitute and appoint
_____ as Agent, as the true and lawful attorney in fact of me and for the use and benefit of
me, as Principal, and to do and perform each and every act hereinafter listed; and, in addition, to ensure as my Agent
and attorney that any health care professional treating me shall comply with my specific instructions listed in Exhibits
A, B, and C attached hereto and made a part hereof by this specific reference thereto, to-wit:

1. **Employ and Discharge Others.** To employ and discharge physicians, psychiatrists, dentists, nurses,
   therapists, and other professionals as you, as Agent, may deem necessary for my physical, mental and
   emotional well-being, and to pay them, or any of them reasonable compensation.

2. **Appoint Guardian and / or Conservator.** To nominate and / or petition for the appointment of you, my
   Agent, or any person you deem appropriate as primary, successor or alternate guardian, guardian ad litem or
   conservator or to any fiduciary office (all of such offices or guardian, et. al. being hereinafter referred to as
   "Personal Representative") representing me or any interest of mine or any person for whom I may have a
   right of duty to nominate or petition for such appointment; to grant to any such Personal Representative all
   of the powers under applicable law that I am permitted to grant; to waive any bond requirement for such
   Personal Representative that I am permitted by law to waive.

3. **Consent or Refuse Consent to My Medical Care.** To give or withhold consent to my medical care,
   surgery, or other medical procedures or tests; to arrange for my hospitalization, convalescent care, or home
   care which I or you, as my Agent, may have previously allowed or consent to which may have been implied
   due to emergency conditions. I ask you to be guided in making such decisions by what I have told you about
   my personal preferences regarding such care. Based on those same preferences, you may also summon
   paramedics or other emergency medical personnel and seek emergency treatment for me, or choose not to
   do so, as you deem appropriate given my wishes and my medical status at the time of the decision.

   You are authorized, when dealing with hospitals and physicians, to sign documents titled or purporting to be
   a "Refusal to Permit Treatment" and "Leaving Hospital Against Medical Advice," as well as any necessary
   waivers of or releases from liability required by the hospitals or physicians to implement my wishes
   regarding medical treatment or non-treatment.

   In addition, you as my Agent and attorney shall have access to any medical records pertaining to my
   physical or mental condition, or any communications, oral or written, from any doctor engaged to treat me.
   Any doctor (i.e. physician, surgeon, osteopath, psychologist or other health care professional) engaged to
   treat me may rely on this Power of Attorney in divulging information as to my mental or physical condition.

4. **Consent or Refuse Consent to my Psychiatric Care.** Upon the execution of a certificate by two (2)
   independent psychiatrists who have examined me, who are licensed to practice in the state of my residence
   and in whose opinion I am in immediate need of hospitalization because of mental disorders, alcoholism, or
   drug abuse, to arrange for my voluntary admission to an appropriate hospital or institution for treatment of
   the diagnosed problem or disorder; to arrange for private psychiatric and psychological care, and to evoke,
   modify, withdraw or change consent to such hospitalization, institutionalization and private treatment which
   I or you, as my Agent, may have given at an earlier time.

5. **Refuse My Life Prolonging Procedures.** To request that aggressive medical therapy not be instituted or be
   discontinued, including (but not limited to) cardiopulmonary resuscitation, the implantation of a cardiac
   pacemaker, renal dialysis, parenteral feeding, the use of respirators or ventilators, blood transfusions,

nasogastric tube use, intravenous feedings, endotracheal tube use, antibiotics, and organ transplants. You should try to discuss the specifics of any decision with me if I am able to communicate with you in any manner, even blinking my eyes. If I am unconscious, comatose, senile or otherwise unreachable by such communication, you should make the decision guided primarily by any preferences which I may have previously expressed, and secondarily by the information given by the physicians treating me as to my medical diagnosis and prognosis. You may specifically request and concur with the writing of a "no-code" (DO NOT RESUSCITATE) order by the attending physician.

6. **Provide Me Relief From Pain**. To consent to and arrange for the administration of pain-relieving drugs of any type or other surgical or medical procedures calculated to relieve my pain even though their use may lead to permanent physical damage, addiction or even hasten the moment of (but not intentionally cause) my death. You may also consent to and arrange for additional pain-relief therapies such as biofeedback, guided imagery, relaxation therapy, acupuncture, or cutaneous stimulation and other therapies which I or you believe may be helpful to me.

7. **Third Party Reliance.** For the purpose of inducing any physician, hospital, bank, broker, custodian, insurer, lender, transfer agent, taxing authority, governmental agency or other party to act in accordance with the powers granted in this document, I hereby represent, warrant and agree that:

   a. If this document is revoked or amended for any reason, I, my estate, my heirs, successors, and assigns will hold such party or parties harmless from any loss suffered or liability incurred by such party or parties in acting in accordance with this document prior to that party's receipt of written notice of any such termination or amendment.

   b. The powers conferred on you by this document may be exercised by you, _____, individually; and your signature or acts under the authority granted in this document may be accepted by third parties as fully authorized by me and with the same force and effect as if I were personally present, competent, and acting on my own behalf.

   c. No person who acts in reliance upon any representation you may make as to the scope of our authority granted under this document shall incur any liability to me, my estate, my heirs, successors or assigns for permitting you to exercise any such power, nor shall any person who deals with you be responsible to determine or ensure the proper applications of funds or property.

   d. You shall have the right to seek appropriate court orders mandating acts which you deem appropriate if a third party refuses to comply with actions taken by you which are authorized by this document, or enjoining acts by third parties which you have not authorized. In addition, you may bring legal action against any third party who fails to comply with actions I have authorized you to take and demand damages, including punitive damages, on my behalf for such noncompliance.

   GIVING AND GRANTING unto you as agent and attorney, full power and authority to do and perform all and every act and thing whatsoever requisite and necessary to be done in and about the premises, as fully to all intents and purposes as I might or could do if personally present, hereby ratifying and confirming all that you, as Agent and attorney, shall lawfully do or cause to be done by virtue of these presents.

   PROVIDED, HOWEVER, that this Power of Attorney shall become effective only upon the disability of _____. Such person shall be deemed to be disabled for the purpose of this Power of Attorney in the event that a qualified physician certifies in writing to _____ that _____ is, by reason of illness or mental or physical disability, unable to give prompt and intelligent consideration to decisions regarding his health care. This Power of Attorney shall thereafter remain in full force and effect until revoked.

In the event this Power is recorded, it may be revoked only by and instrument revoking the same, duly acknowledged by me and recorded in the same county or counties in which this power was originally recorded.

The following is a specimen of the signature of the Agent and attorney hereby appointed, to wit:

_____

IN WITNESS WHEREOF, I, _____ have executed this instrument on the _____ day of _____, 1995

_____

S. S. Number: _____

_____ Witness

_____ Witness

STATE OF ARIZONA   )

) ss.

    County of Maricopa   )

        I, the undersigned Notary Public, **DO HEREBY CERTIFY** that
_____, personally known to me to be the same person whose name is subscribed to the foregoing instrument, and appearing to me to be of sound mind and free from duress at the time of execution of this Medical Power of Attorney, came before me this day in person and acknowledged that he signed the said instrument as his free and voluntary act, for the uses and purposes therein set forth.

        GIVEN under my hand and notarial seal, this ___ day of _____, 1995.

_____

NOTARY PUBLIC

My Commission Expires:

_____

<u>MEDICAL POWER OF ATTORNEY</u>

_____EXHIBIT A

I HEREBY DECLARE THAT IN THE EVENT AT ANY TIME, ANY OF THE FOLLOWING SITUATIONS SHALL OCCUR:

1) **I AM IN A COMA WITH NO CHANCE OF REGAINING CONSCIOUSNESS; OR**
2) **I AM IN A COMA WITH A SMALL CHANCE OF REGAINING CONSCIOUSNESS; OR**
3) **I HAVE IRREVERSIBLE BRAIN DAMAGE, UNABLE TO RECOGNIZE PEOPLE OR SPEAK; OR**
4) **I HAVE IRREVERSIBLE BRAIN DAMAGE, PLUS TERMINAL DISEASE;**

THEN MY DESIRES SHALL BE AS FOLLOWS, TO-WIT:

	I want	I want treatment tried. If no clear improvement stop	I am undecided	I do not want
CARDIOPULMONARY RESUSCITATION If at the point of death, using drugs and electric shock to keep the heart beating; artificial breathing.		N/A		
MECHANICAL BREATHING Breathing by machine.				
ARTIFICIAL NUTRITION AND HYDRATION Giving nutrition and fluid through a tube in the veins, nose, or stomach.				
MAJOR SURGERY Such as removing the gall bladder or part of the intestines.		N/A		
KIDNEY DIALYSIS Cleaning the blood by machine or by fluid passed through the belly.				
CHEMOTHERAPY Using drugs to fight cancer.				
MINOR SURGERY Such as removing some tissue from an infected area		N/A		
INVASIVE DIAGNOSTIC TESTS Such as using a flexible tube to look into the stomach.		N/A		
BLOOD OR BLOOD PRODUCTS Such as receiving transfusions.				
ANTIBIOTICS Using drugs to fight infection.				
SIMPLE DIAGNOSTIC TESTS Such as performing blood tests, MRI or CAT scans.		N/A		
PAIN MEDICATIONS EVEN IF THEY DULL CONSCIOUSNESS AND INDIRECTLY SHORTEN MY LIFE				

MEDICAL POWER OF ATTORNEY

_____ **EXHIBIT B**

(Under Arizona Law, an autopsy may be required)

If you wish to do so, reflect your desires below:

_____ 1. **I DO NOT** consent to an autopsy

_____ 2. **I CONSENT** to an autopsy

_____ 3. My Agent **MAY** give consent to **OR REFUSE** an autopsy

MEDICAL POWER OF ATTORNEY

_____ **EXHIBIT C**

Under Arizona law, you may make a gift of all or part of your body to a bank or storage
facility or a hospital, physician or medical or dental school for transplantation, therapy, medical or dental
evaluation or research for the advancement of medical or dental science. You may also authorize your Agent to
do so, or a member of your family may make a gift unless you give them notice that you do not want a gift
made. In the space below, you may make a gift yourself or state that you do not want to make a gift. If you do
not complete this section, your Agent will have the authority to make a gift of a part of your body pursuant to
law.

If any of the statements below reflects your desire, initial on the line next to that statement. **YOU DO
NOT HAVE TO INITIAL ANY OF THE STATEMENTS.**

_____ **I DO NOT WANT TO MAKE AN ORGAN OR TISSUE DONATION AND
I DO NOT WANT MY AGENT OR FAMILY TO DO SO.**

_____ **I HAVE ALREADY SIGNED A WRITTEN AGREEMENT OR DONOR
CARD REGARDING ORGAN AND TISSUE DONATION WITH THE
FOLLOWING INDIVIDUAL OR INSTITUTION:**

_____

_____ **PURSUANT TO ARIZONA LAW, I HEREBY GIVE, EFFECTIVE ON
DEATH:**

[ ] **Any needed organ or parts.**

[ ] **The following parts or organs listed:**

_____

_____

_____

FOR (CHECK ONE):

[ ] **Any legally authorized purpose.**

[ ] **Transplant or therapeutic purposes only.**

The form below is a wallet-sized "Notice in Case of Accident or Other Emergency." Make a copy of it, fill it out, and keep it in your wallet with your driver's license and insurance cards so that law enforcement and medical personnel will know that you have completed health care forms.

NOTICE: in Case of Accident or Other Emergency:

NAME:_____

DATE:_____

I have signed the following forms: (check)
( ) **Durable Health Care Power of Attorney**
( ) **Living Will**
( ) **Pre-hospital Medical Directives (Do Not Resuscitate)**
( ) **Durable Mental Health Care Power of Attorney**
( ) **Durable General Power of Attorney (Financial)**

Please contact the following for a copy:
Name: _____
Telephone: _____

ADVANCE DIRECTIVES BY STATE

Initially I contacted the attorney general in all fifty states, with the idea that I would include all the living will forms necessary in each state. I soon found out, however, that this book would be extremely long if I were to include all the forms, so I have taken the important items in each state's statute regarding living wills and medical power of attorney and listed them below. Because laws tend to change from time to time, *I strongly recommend that you contact the attorney general in your state to obtain the proper forms before filling them out and distributing them.* For most states they are available to download on the Internet.

Almost all states have a law stipulating that in order to have a legal advance directive, a person must be eighteen years or older. Almost all states also have a law that the advance directive is invalid if a person is pregnant. Almost all states require two witnesses and/or a notary public to sign the advanced directive before it is declared legal; some states require both.

Below you will find the advance directive requirements for all fifty states in the United States of America:

Alabama: Must be nineteen years old. Advance directives for health care need two witnesses. Witnesses must not be related by blood, adoption, or marriage and not entitled to any part of the estate. Not valid in case of pregnancy.

Alaska: The Alaska Advance Directive document is in five parts:

- Part I—Durable power of attorney for health care: signed by two witnesses known to you and present when you sign or acknowledge your signature, or signed before a notary public
- Part II—Specific instructions for end-of-life health care. Needs no witnesses
- Part III—Instruction to make an anatomical gift following death
- Part IV—Advance decisions about mental health treatment
- Part V—Designation of a physician to have primary responsibility for your health care

Arizona: Witness OR notary is required for a living will; same for a health care power of attorney (proxy). Witness must be eighteen years or older; cannot be related by blood, adoption, or marriage; cannot be entitled to any part of your estate; cannot be appointed as representative or involved in providing your health care at the time this document is signed.

Arizona has another form called Pre Hospital Medical Care Directive (DO NOT RESUSCITATE). **IMPORTANT:** This document must be on paper with an orange background. This document, signed by you and your doctor, informs emergency medical technicians (EMTs) or hospital emergency personnel not to resuscitate.

Arkansas: Arkansas Advance Directive consists of two documents:

- Arkansas Declaration
- Arkansas Durable Power of Attorney for Health

The law requires signing before two witnesses, who must also sign to attest that documents were filled out voluntarily. Witnesses must be at least eighteen years of age and cannot be a person who is selected as health care proxy. Not valid in case of pregnancy.

California: An advance health care directive is now the legally recognized format for a living will and a durable power of attorney for health care. A DPAHC executed before 1992 has expired and should be replaced. Not valid in case of pregnancy. A durable power of attorney for health care (proxy) requires two witnesses OR a notary. You must be eighteen years old (or an emancipated minor). Any adult member of your family (e.g., spouse, adult child), friend, or someone else you trust may be appointed as agent (proxy). The law prohibits choosing one's doctor, or a person who operates a community care facility or a residential care facility in which you receive care.

Colorado: Colorado has two documents: the living will and the medical durable power of attorney.
- Declaration as to medical or surgical treatment (living will) requires two witnesses but is not valid in case of pregnancy. The living will does not go into effect unless two doctors declare a person has a terminal condition.
- Medical durable power of attorney for health care (proxy) does not require any witnesses or notary.

The following cannot witness or sign a living will: patients in a facility in which one is receiving care; any doctor or employee of one's doctor; any employee of the facility or agency providing one's care; any creditors or people who may inherit one's money or property.

A CPR directive allows you, your agent, guardian, or proxy to refuse resuscitation. This directive must be signed by a doctor.

Connecticut: In Connecticut there are three types of advance directives:
(1) the living will or health care instructions; (2) the appointment of a health care agent; and (3) the appointment of an attorney-in-fact for health care decisions, also called a durable power of attorney for health care.

Your attorney-in-fact may make decisions about any aspect of your medical treatment except in three areas: (1) withdrawal of life-support systems; (2) withdrawal of food and fluids; and (3) medical treatment designed solely to maintain your physical comfort. The attorney-in-fact form should be notarized.

You must sign the document in the presence of two witnesses in order for any of the different types of advance directives to be valid. The witnesses then sign the form. The person who you appoint to be your health care agent, or as your conservator, cannot be a witness to your signature of the appointment form. Otherwise, except in a few unique situations, Connecticut law does not state who may or may not be a witness to your advance directive.

Delaware: The Delaware Advanced Directive includes provisions for both living will and health care proxy on one form. Two witnesses required. Although signing this form in front of a notary public is not legally required, it is advisable.

CAUTION: Agent's Authority (taken from the Delaware Advance Directive form): "I grant to my agent full authority to make decisions for me regarding my health care; provided that, in exercising this authority, my Agent shall follow my desires as stated in my Advance Directives document or otherwise known to my Agent. Accordingly, my agent is authorized as follows:
- To consent to, refuse, or withdraw consent to any and all types of medical care, treatment, surgical procedures, diagnostic procedures, medication, and the use of mechanical or other procedures that affect any bodily function

- To have access to medical records and information to the same extent that I am entitled to, including the right to disclose the contents to others
- To authorize my admission to or discharge from any hospital, nursing home, residential care, assisted living, or similar facility or service
- To contract for any health care related service or facility on my behalf. Without my agent incurring personal financial liability for such contracts
- To hire and fire medical, social service, and other support personnel responsible for my care
- To authorize, or refuse to authorize, any medication or procedure intended to relieve pain, even though such use may lead to physical damage, addiction, or hasten the moment of (but not intentionally cause) my death

My Agent's authority becomes effective when my attending physician determines I lack the capacity to make my own "health care decisions."

District of Columbia: The District of Columbia Declaration consists of a living will, which needs two witnesses, and a power of attorney for health care (proxy) which also needs two witnesses. These witnesses cannot:
- Be the person who signed the declaration on your behalf and at your direction
- Be related to you by blood or marriage
- Stand to inherit from your estate upon your death
- Be directly financially responsible for your medical care
- Be your attending doctor or an employee of your attending doctor
- Be an employee of a health care facility in which you are a patient

Your declaration does not have to be notarized. Before the durable power of attorney for health care can go into effect, two physicians licensed to practice in the District of Columbia, including one psychiatrist, must certify in writing that you are mentally unable to make health care decisions.

Florida: Two witnesses are needed for both a living will and a designation of a health care surrogate (proxy). At least one person must not be a husband or wife or a blood relative of the principal.

Georgia: Living will and power of attorney require two witnesses. Living will is not valid in case of pregnancy. Neither witness can be a person:
- Who is your Healthcare agent
- Who will knowingly inherit anything from you or otherwise gain a financial benefit from your death
- Who is directly involved in your health care

Not more than one witness can be an employee, agent, or medical staff member of the health care facility in which you are receiving health care.
Georgia Advanced Directives for Healthcare do not have to be notarized.

Hawaii: Living will (declaration) needs two witnesses and a notary but is not valid in case of pregnancy. Two witnesses and/or a notary are also required for a durable power of attorney for health care decisions (proxy). This form has four parts:
- Power of attorney for health care
- Living will, which lets you give specific instructions about any aspect of your health care
- Instructions about your wishes for organ donation
- Provision to designate a physician to have primary responsibility for your health care

Idaho: Idaho Advanced Directives packet contains two legal documents: the Idaho Living Will and the Idaho Durable Power of Attorney for Healthcare. These documents protect your right to refuse medical treatments you do not want, or to request treatment you do want, in the event you lose the ability to make decisions yourself.
Idaho law also provides for the preparation of a Physician Orders for Scope of Treatment (POST) form, which is appropriate in cases where a patient has an incurable or irreversible injury, disease, illness or condition, or is in a persistent vegetative state. It is similar to a DNR (do not resuscitate) order, but broader. It must be obtained from, and signed by, your physician. If there is a conflict between the instructions included in an individual's POST and living will, the orders of the POST will be followed.
Idaho law requires that you sign your living will, and /or your durable power of attorney, though you do not have to have it witnessed; however, it is a good idea to sign it in front of a witness who also signs it.
You do not need to notarize your Idaho Declaration or Durable Power of Attorney.

Illinois: Living will requires two witnesses. Not valid in case of pregnancy. One witness required for power of attorney for health care (proxy).
The living will, unlike a health care power of attorney, applies only if you have a terminal condition. Even if you sign a living will, food and water cannot be withheld if their absence would be the only cause of death.

If you have both a health care power of attorney and a living will, the agent you name in the power of attorney will make your health care decisions unless he/she is unavailable.

Your health care agent cannot be your health care professional or other health care provider. And your agent should not be the witness to your signing of these documents.

Indiana: The Indiana Advance Directive consists of three documents:
- The Indiana Power of Attorney for Healthcare Decisions and Appointment of Healthcare Representative
- The Indiana Living Will Declaration
- The Indiana Life-Prolonging Procedures Declaration

The Indiana Power of Attorney for Healthcare Decisions lets you name someone to make decisions about your medical care—including decisions about life support—if you can no longer speak for yourself. The law requires that you sign this document in the presence of a notary public.

The Indiana Living Will lets you refuse life-prolonging procedures in the event that you develop a terminal condition and can no longer make your own medical decisions. The declaration goes into effect only when your doctor certifies in writing that you have an injury, disease, or illness from which, to a reasonable degree of medical certainty, there can be no recovery, and death will occur within a short period of time without the use of life- prolonging procedures. State law requires that you sign this document in front of two competent witnesses. You do not need to notarize this document.

The Indiana Life-Prolonging Procedures Declaration lets you request the use of all life-prolonging procedures in the event you develop a terminal condition and can no longer make your own medical decisions. The law requires that you sign this document, or direct another to sign it, in the presence of two competent witnesses, eighteen years of age or older, who must also sign the document to attest that they personally know you and believe you to be of sound mind. You do not need to notarize this declaration.

Iowa: In Iowa there are two documents that protect your right to refuse medical treatment you do not want, or to request treatments you do want in the event you lose the ability to make decisions for yourself. The two documents are the Iowa Durable Power of Attorney for Healthcare and the Iowa Declaration (Living Will).

Two witnesses or a notary are required for a living will. Not valid in the case of pregnancy.

Power of attorney for health care (proxy) requires two witnesses OR a notary public.

The witnesses cannot be:
- Your doctor or other treating health care provider
- An employee of your treating health care provider
- An individual who is less than eighteen years of age

The agent you have selected for the durable power of attorney for health care cannot be a witness to that document.

Kansas: The Kansas Advance Directive for Healthcare consists of two parts: the living will, and a health care proxy.
- The living will lets you discuss your wishes about medical care in the event that you develop a terminal condition, are permanently unconscious, and can no longer make your own medical decisions.
- The health care proxy lets you name someone to make decisions about your medical care, including decisions about life-sustaining treatment, if you can no longer speak for yourself. This document will be legally binding only if the person completing it is a competent adult.

The law requires that you sign your document, or direct someone else to sign it, in the presence of two witnesses who must be at least eighteen years old. The witnesses must also sign the document. Your witnesses cannot be:
- Your appointed health care proxy
- Related to you by blood, adoption, or marriage
- Entitled to any portion of your estate upon your death, either through your will or under the laws of intestate succession
- Someone directly financially responsible for your medical care

The law also requires that your appointed health care proxy and alternate health care proxy sign and date the document.

You do not need your document notarized.

Kentucky: The Kentucky Living Will Directive Act of 1994 was passed to insure that citizens have the right to make decisions regarding their own medical care. The living will allows you to leave instructions in four critical areas:
- Designate a health care surrogate
- Refuse or request life-prolonging treatment
- Refuse or request artificial feeding or hydration (tube feeding)
- Express your wishes regarding organ donation

Everyone age eighteen or older can have a living will. However, it is not valid in the case of pregnancy. Kentucky law (KRS 311.615) actually specifies the form you should fill out.

The living-will form includes two sections:

- A health care surrogate section, which allows you to designate one or more persons, such as a family member or close friend, to make health care decisions for you if you lose the ability to decide for yourself.
- A living-will section, in which you may make your wishes known regarding life-prolonging treatment so that your health care surrogate or doctor will know what you want them to do. You can also decide whether to donate any of your organs in the event or your death.

The law requires that you sign your document, or direct another to sign it, in the presence of two witnesses who must be at least nineteen years of age. These witnesses must also sign the document to show that they personally know you, believe you are of sound mind, that they did not sign the document on your behalf, and that they do not fall into one of the categories of people who cannot be witnesses, namely:

- Your appointed health care proxy
- People related to you by blood, adoption, or marriage
- People entitled to any portion of your estate, either through your will, under Kentucky descent and distribution statutes, or under the laws of intestate succession
- Your attending physician, or an employee of a health care facility in which you are a patient or resident, unless the employee serves as a notary public
- Someone directly financially responsible for your medical care

Louisiana: The Louisiana Declaration is the state's living will. It lets you state your wishes about medical care in the event that you become terminally and irreversibly ill and can no longer make your own medical decisions.

In addition, this declaration lets you designate another person to decide whether life-sustaining treatment should be withheld or withdrawn in the event you become terminally and irreversibly ill and can no longer make your own medical decisions.

This document will be legally binding only if the person completing it is a competent adult (at least eighteen years old).

The law requires that you sign your declaration in the presence of two competent adult witnesses, who must also sign the document to show that they personally know you and believe you to be of sound mind.

These witnesses cannot be:

- Related to you by blood or marriage
- Entitled to any portion of your estate

This document does not need notarization.

Maine: The Maine Advance Directive protects your right to refuse medical treatment you do not want, or to request treatment you do want, in the event you lose the ability to make decisions yourself. The document is divided into two sections:

- Power of attorney for health care lets you name someone to make decisions about your medical care—including decisions about life support—if you can no longer speak for yourself.
- Instructions for health care. This functions as your Maine living will. It lets you state your wishes about the withholding or withdrawal of medical care in the event you can no longer speak for yourself.

The law requires that you sign your advance directive in front of two witnesses. Although the law does not restrict who can serve as a witness, it is suggested that your witnesses be at least eighteen years of age and that your health care agent not act as a witness.

Maryland: The Maryland Advance Directive protects your right to refuse medical treatment you do not want or to request treatment you do want in the event you lose the ability to make decisions for yourself. The document is divided into two parts:

- The appointment of health care agent, which lets you name someone to make decisions about your medical care—including decisions about life support—if you can no longer make those decisions yourself.
- The advance medical directive. These are instructions that function as Maryland's living will. The directive lets you state your wishes about medical care in the event you can no longer make your own medical decisions.

The law requires that you sign Part A of your advance directive in the presence of two witnesses. The person you name as your agent cannot serve as a witness. At least one of your witnesses must be a person who is not entitled to any portion of your estate and who is not entitled to any financial benefit by reason of your death.

You do not need to notarize your Maryland advance directive.

Massachusetts: The state has no provision for a living will. The Massachusetts Health Care Proxy lets you name someone to make decisions about your medical care—including decisions about life support—if you can no longer speak for yourself. Two adult witnesses are required for a health care proxy and must sign the document. The person you select as your proxy cannot sign as a witness. This document does not have to be notarized.

Michigan: The state has no provision for a living will; however, the Michigan Designation of Patient Advocate for Healthcare lets you name someone to make decisions about your medical care—including decisions about life support, mental health treatment, and anatomical gifts—if you can no longer speak for yourself. The law requires that you sign your document before two witnesses. These witnesses cannot be:

- Your spouse, parent, child, grandchild, or sibling
- A person who stands to inherit from your estate, either by law or through a will
- A physician or patient advocate
- An employee of your life or health insurance provider
- An employee of your treating health care facility, or mental health care facility
- An employee of a home for the aged, if you are a patient in that facility

You do not have to have this document notarized in the state of Michigan.

Minnesota: The Minnesota Health Care Directive is in two parts:

- Appointment of a health care agent. This lets you name someone to make decisions about your health care—including decisions about life support—if you can no longer speak for yourself, or immediately, if you so specify in the document.
- Health care instructions. This part functions as your living will and lets you state your wishes about medical care in the event that you can no longer make your own medical decisions. You must be a competent adult at least eighteen years of age. In order to make this document legally binding, you have two options: (1) sign it in the presence of two witnesses who are eighteen years of age or older, and not the person you pick to be your agent or alternate agent; or (2) sign it in the presence of a notary public.

Mississippi: The Mississippi Advance Healthcare Directive consists of four parts:

- Part I—Power of attorney for health care. This part lets you name someone to make decisions about your health care—including decisions about life support—if you can no longer speak for yourself, or immediately if you so specify.
- Part II—Instructions for health care, which functions as your living will. It lets you state your wishes about health care in the event that you can no longer speak for yourself.
- Part III—An optional section that lets you specify your primary physician.

- Part IV—Certificate of authorization for organ donation. This is also an optional section.

In order for this document to be legal, you must sign it before two witnesses, who must also sign to attest that they personally know you and that you are of sound mind and under no duress. These witnesses cannot include

- The person you appointed as your agent
- Your health care provider, or an employee of your health care provider or facility

Or, you can sign your document in the presence of a notary public.

Missouri: The Missouri Advance Directive consists of two documents that protect your right to refuse medical treatment you do not want or to request treatment you do want, in the event you cannot speak for yourself:

- Part I—The Missouri Durable Power of Attorney for Healthcare lets you name someone to make decisions about your health care—including decisions about life support.
- Part II—The Missouri Declaration is your state's living will. It lets you specify your wishes about medical care in the event that you develop a terminal condition and can no longer make your own treatment decisions. The declaration becomes effective only if your death would occur even with the use of life-sustaining treatment.

You must be at least eighteen years old to fill out these documents.

The law requires that you sign your durable power of attorney for health care in the presence of a notary public.

Montana: The Montana Advance Directive contains two legal documents that protect your right to refuse medical treatment you do not want, or to request treatment that you do want, in the event that you lose the ability to make your own decisions.

- The Montana Appointment of an Agent lets you name someone to make decisions about life-sustaining treatment if you are in a terminal condition and can no longer speak for yourself. The term "terminal condition" means an incurable or irreversible condition that, without the administration of life-sustaining treatment, will, in the opinion of your doctor or advanced-practice registered nurse, result in death within a relatively short time.
- The Montana Declaration is your state's living will. It lets you state your wishes about medical care in the event that you develop a terminal condition and can no longer make your own medical decisions.

The law requires that you sign your appointment of an agent in the presence of two witnesses, at least eighteen years of age, who must also sign the document to attest that you voluntarily signed the document in their presence.

There are no restrictions on who may act as a witness, but it is recommended that you do not use your agent as one of them.

You do not need to have this document signed before a notary public.

Nebraska: The Nebraska Advance Directive consists of two documents:
- The Nebraska Power of Attorney for Healthcare
- The Nebraska Declaration

These documents must be signed in front of two witnesses or before a notary public. The documents will be legal only if the person completing them is a competent adult (at least nineteen years of age) or someone who is or has been married.

The person you appoint as your attorney-in-fact cannot be:
- Your doctor; or an employee of your doctor who is not related to you by blood, marriage, or adoption
- An owner, operator, or employee of your treating health care provider who is not related to you by blood, marriage or adoption
- A person unrelated to you by blood, marriage, or adoption who is currently serving as an attorney-in-fact for ten or more people

Nevada: The Nevada Advance Directive consists of two documents:
- The Nevada Durable Power of Attorney for Health care Decisions. This document requires a notary or two witnesses.
- The Nevada Declaration, which is the state's living will. This document also requires two witnesses.

These witnesses cannot be:
- The person you name as your agent
- A health care provider
- An employee of a health care provider
- An operator of a community care facility
- An employee of an operator of a health care facility

Due to restrictions in Nevada law, your health care agent does not have the power to authorize any of the following:
- Abortion
- Sterilization
- Commitment or placement in a facility for treatment of mental illness
- Convulsive treatment
- Psychosurgery

- Aversive intervention

New Hampshire: New Hampshire Advance Directive consists of two documents:
- The New Hampshire Durable Power of Attorney for Healthcare
- The New Hampshire Declaration, which is your state's living will.

Both must be signed by a notary or justice of the peace OR two witnesses.

The documents will be legal only if the person completing them is a competent adult at least eighteen years of age.

If you want to give your health care agent power to withhold or withdraw medically administered nutrition and hydration, you must say so in your directive. Otherwise, your health care agent will not be able to direct that.

Under no conditions will your agent be able to direct the withholding of food and drink that you are able to eat and drink normally.

Unless you state otherwise, your health care agent will have the same power to make decisions about your health care as you would have had, if those decisions are made consistent with state law.

New Jersey: The New Jersey Advance Directive comes in two parts:
- Part I—Permits the appointment of a health care representative to make decisions about life-sustaining treatment if you no longer can make those decisions.
- Part II—Your state's living will. It lets you provide instruction and directions regarding your wishes about medical care in the event that you develop a terminal condition or are permanently unconscious and can no longer make your own decisions.

You may use either one or both of these documents. The document will be legally binding only if you are a competent adult.

Either instruction directives or appointment of a health care representative needs two witnesses or notary public. You need to notarize your advance directive only if you cannot directly sign the advance directive yourself.

You can appoint a family member, including, but not limited to, your spouse or domestic partner or a close friend, as your health care agent whom you trust to make serious decisions.

If you designate your spouse as your agent, unless otherwise specified in the advance directive, his or her authority is automatically revoked upon divorce or separation.

If it is your domestic partner, his or her authority is revoked upon termination of your domestic partnership, unless otherwise stated in your advance directive.

Before your agent can make decisions on your behalf, your doctor or treating health care institution must receive a copy of the Appointment of Healthcare Representative, and your attending physician and one other doctor must confirm that you are unable to make health care decisions.

New Mexico: The New Mexico Advance Healthcare Directive consists of two parts:
- Part I—Power of attorney for health care
- Part II—Instructions for health care, which functions as your state's living will.
- There is an optional section that allows you to designate a physician to have primary responsibility for your health care

These instructions for health care require no witnesses. However, witnesses are recommended to avoid concerns that this document might be forged, that you were forced to sign it, or that it does not genuinely represent your wishes.

These documents are legally binding only if the person completing them is a competent adult or an emancipated minor between the ages of sixteen and eighteen who has been married, who is on active duty in the armed forces, or who has been declared by court order to be emancipated.

New York: The New York Advance Directive consists of two legal documents that protect your right to refuse medical treatment. You may use either one or both of these documents:
- The New York Healthcare Proxy, which lets you name someone to make health care decisions for you, including decisions about life support. You must be eighteen years of age or older to make these documents legal. You must sign your health care proxy document before two adult witnesses. Your health care proxy cannot be one of the witnesses.
- The New York Living Will, which lets you state your wishes about medical care in the event you develop an irreversible condition that prevents you from making your own decisions. The New York Living Will is authorized by law created by New York courts, not by legislation, therefore there are no specific requirements guiding its use, and it does not have to be signed before witnesses or notarized.

North Carolina: The North Carolina Advance Directive contains two legal documents that protect your rights to refuse medical treatment:
- The North Carolina Healthcare Power of Attorney is a form that gives the person you designate as your health care agent broad powers to make health care decisions for you when you cannot make the decisions yourself.

- The North Carolina Advance Directive for Natural Death (Living Will) is a form you can use to give instructions for the future if you want your health care providers to withhold or withdraw life-prolonging measures in certain situations. This form is intended to be valid in any jurisdiction in which it is presented, but other states may impose different requirements.

The North Carolina Declaration of Desire for a Natural Death and the Healthcare Power of Attorney require two witnesses *and* a notary public.

North Dakota: The North Dakota Statutory Healthcare Directive lets you name someone to make decisions for your medical care—including decisions about life support—if you can no longer make those decisions. The person you name as your agent should clearly understand your wishes and be willing to accept the responsibility of making medical decisions for you. Your agent may be a family member or a close friend you trust to make serious decisions. In order to make this document legally binding, you must sign it, or direct someone else to sign for you, in the presence of two witnesses or a notary, who must also sign the document.

The witnesses and the notary public cannot:
- Be your spouse or be related to you by blood, marriage, or adoption
- Stand to inherit from your estate upon your death
- Have any claim against your estate at the time you sign the document
- Be your doctor
- Be directly financially responsible for your medical care

If two witnesses are signing your health care directive, at least one witness cannot be a health care provider giving direct care or an employee of the health care provider giving you direct care.

Ohio: The Ohio Advance Directive consists of two legal documents relating to your medical treatment if you no longer can make medical decisions:
- The Ohio Durable Power of Attorney for Healthcare lets you name someone to make decisions about your health care—including decisions about life support—if you can no longer speak for yourself.
- The Ohio Living Will Declaration lets you state your wishes about medical care in the event that you become terminally ill or permanently unconscious and can no longer make your own medical decisions. The declaration becomes effective if your doctor determines that you are terminally ill and your death would occur without the use of life-sustaining medical care. One other doctor must agree with your attending physician's opinion of your medical condition.

The signing of both these documents must either be witnessed by a notary public or signed in the presence of two adult witnesses who must also sign the documents to make them legal. These witnesses cannot be:
- Related to you by blood, marriage, or adoption
- The person you appoint as your agent
- Your doctor
- The administrator of the nursing home in which you are receiving care

Under Ohio law, if you are in a terminal condition or a permanently unconscious state, your living will declaration will have control over a health care power of attorney if there is any conflict.

Oklahoma: The Oklahoma Advance Directive for Healthcare has three sections:
- Section I—The living will, which lets you state your wishes about medical care in the event that you can no longer make your own medical decisions and you are terminally ill or persistently unconscious
- Section II—The appointment of a health care proxy, which lets you name someone to make decisions about your medical care if you can no longer speak for yourself
- Section III—A provision for anatomical gifts, which allows you to indicate whether you want to donate any or all of your organs and tissues, or your whole body, for transplantation or other uses after your death.

Your advance directive must be signed before two witnesses, and they must in turn sign it declaring that you are a competent adult eighteen years of age or older.

Oregon: The Oregon Advance Directive consists of three parts:
- Part A—Contains important information that you should read before completing your document.
- Part B—Provides for the appointment of a health care representative who makes decisions about your medical care—including decisions about life support—if you can no longer speak for yourself.
- Part C—Provides for health care instructions; this section serves as your living will. It lets you state your wishes about medical care in the event that you are terminally ill, permanently unconscious, or have an advanced progressive illness and can no longer make your own medical decisions. One other physician must agree with your attending physician's opinion of your medical condition.

The law requires that you sign your document, or direct another to sign it, in the presence of two witnesses, neither of whom may be your attending physician or your health care representative or alternate. Your witnesses must also sign the document to show that they personally know you or have been provided with proof of your identity. If you are a patient in a long-term facility, one of your witnesses must be a person designated by your facility and qualified under the rules of the Department of Human Resources.

Your Oregon Advance Directive does not have to be notarized.

Pennsylvania: The Pennsylvania Advance Directive is a legal document that protects your right to refuse medical treatment you do not want, or to request treatment you do want, in the event you lose the ability to make these decisions by yourself. The Pennsylvania directive is your state's living will. It lets you specify your wishes about medical care in the event that you develop a terminal condition or enter a state of permanent unconsciousness and can no longer make your own medical decisions. The living will becomes effective when your doctor receives a copy of it and determines that you are incompetent and in an end-stage medical condition or a state of permanent unconsciousness.

In your directive you can name another person, called a health care agent or proxy, to make decisions about your medical care—including decisions about life support—when you can no longer make those decisions.

To make your directive legally binding, you must date and sign it, or direct another to sign it, in the presence of two witnesses who must also sign the document to show you knowingly and voluntarily signed the document. You do not need to have your document notarized.

Rhode Island: The Rhode Island Advance Directive consists of two legal documents that protect your right to refuse medical treatment in the event that you lose the ability to make those decisions.

- The Rhode Island Durable Power of Attorney for Healthcare lets you name someone to make decisions about your medical care—including decisions regarding life support—if you cannot speak for yourself.
- The Rhode Island Declaration is your state's living will. It lets you state your wishes about medical care should you develop an incurable or irreversible condition and can no longer make your own decisions. The declaration becomes valid if, in your doctor's opinion, your death would occur without the use of life-sustaining medical care.

The law requires that you sign and date both of these directives in the presence of two witnesses or a notary public. The witnesses then must sign the document to attest that they know you and believe you to be of sound mind and under no duress, fraud, or undue influence. These documents are not valid in the case of pregnancy and if the fetus could develop for a live birth.

South Carolina: The South Carolina Advance Directive consists of two legal documents that protect your right to refuse medical treatment you do not want, or request treatment you do want, in the event you cannot make those decisions yourself:
- The South Carolina Healthcare Power of Attorney lets you name someone to make decisions about your medical care—including life-support decisions if you can no longer speak for yourself.
- The South Carolina Declaration of a Desire for a Natural Death is your state's living will, which allows you to specify your wishes about medical care in the event that you develop a terminal condition or are in a state of permanent unconsciousness and can no longer make your own medical decisions. The declaration becomes effective if your death would occur without the use of life-sustaining medical care. One other doctor must concur with your attending physician's opinion of your medical condition.

The declaration of a desire for a natural death requires two witnesses and a notary. Health care power of attorney requires two witnesses.

South Dakota: The South Dakota Advance Directive consists of two documents related to your refusal of medical treatment or your request for treatment you do want in the event that you cannot make these decisions for yourself:
- The South Dakota Durable Power of Attorney for Healthcare lets you name someone to make decisions about your medical care—including life-support decisions—if you can no longer make these decisions.
- The South Dakota Living Will Declaration lets you state your wishes about medical care, or the lack thereof, should you no longer be able to make these decisions. The living will goes into effect if your attending physician determines that you are in a terminal condition, death is imminent, and you are no longer able to communicate decisions about your medical care.

The living will declaration requires two witnesses. It is not valid in the case of pregnancy. The durable power of attorney needs two witnesses or a notary.

Tennessee: The Tennessee Advance Directive consists of two legal documents:
- The appointment of a health care agent, which requires two witnesses. You and the witnesses must sign the document. A notary is optional.
- The advance care plan, which also requires two witnesses. You and the witnesses must sign the document

Texas: The Texas Advance Directive consists of two legal documents: the Texas Medical Power of Attorney and the Texas Directive to Physicians and Family or

Surrogates (Living Will). In order to make these directives legal, you must sign them in the presence of two witnesses who must also sign.

For the Texas Medical Power of Attorney, at least one witness cannot be:
- The person whom you name as your agent
- Related to you by blood or marriage
- An employee of a health care facility in which you are a patient if she or he is involved with your care
- An officer, director, or business office employee of the health care facility or a parent organization of the health care facility
- A person entitled to any part of your estate upon your death either by will or operation of law.
- Any other person who has a claim against your estate at the time you sign the medical power of attorney.

For the Texas Directive to Physicians, at least one of the witnesses cannot be:
- Designated by you to make a treatment decision
- Related to you by blood or marriage
- Entitled to any part of your estate after your death under a will or by operation of law
- Your doctor or an employee of your doctor
- An employee of a health care facility in which you are a patient
- An officer, director, partner, or business office employee of the health care facility or any parent organization of the health care facility
- A person who, at the time you sign the directive, has a claim against your estate after your death

You do not have to have either document notarized.

Utah: The Utah Advance Healthcare Directive is divided into four parts:
- Part I—Allows you to appoint a surrogate decision maker to make medical-treatment decisions on your behalf. This part of the document goes into effect whenever your attending physician certifies that you are unable to make an informed decision about receiving or refusing health care.
- Part II—Lets you state your wishes about medical care in the event that your attending physician certifies that you are unable to make an informed decision about receiving or refusing health care.
- Part III—Tells you how to revoke your directive.
- Part IV—Makes your directive legal. Your directive can be oral or written. In order to make it legal it must be witnessed by an individual eighteen years of age or older. If you are physically unable to sign the directive, you may arrange to have someone else sign it in your presence at your direction.

Your witness cannot be:

- Related to you by blood or marriage
- Entitled to any portion of your estate according to the laws of intestate succession of Utah or under any will or codicil
- Directly financially responsible for your medical care
- A health care provider who is providing care to you or an administrator at a health care facility in which you are receiving care
- The person you have designated to be your agent or alternate agent

Your directive does not have to be notarized.

Vermont: The Vermont Advance Directive for Healthcare is a legal document that consists of nine parts. You can fill out any or all of the parts. You may also use any advance directive form or format as long as it is properly signed and witnessed. The directive can include instructions about your health care as well as what should happen with your body after you die.

- You have the right to consent to or refuse any medical treatment
- You have the right to appoint an agent to make decisions for you
- You may use this directive to share your wishes in advance (living will)

You can revoke or suspend your advance directive at any time, unless you expressly waive your right to do so.

When you sign your advance directive you must have two adult witnesses. Neither witness can be your spouse, agent, brother, sister, child, grandchild, or reciprocal beneficiary.

Your health care or residential care provider and their staff can be witnesses of advance directives.

Virginia: The Virginia Advance Medical Directive lets you state your wishes about medical care in the event you develop a terminal condition, meaning it is probable that you will not recover from the condition and either your death is imminent or you are in a persistent vegetative state.

The document also lets you name someone to make health care decisions on your behalf anytime you are unable to make your own decisions, not only at the end of life.

State law specifies that you must have your advance medical directive signed before two adult witnesses. Your doctor and/or health care facility personnel can in good faith be witnesses.

Washington: The Washington Advance Directive consists of two legal documents that protect your right to refuse treatment or request treatment in the event you lose the ability to make decisions:

- Document I—The Washington Durable Power of Attorney for Healthcare, which lets you name someone to make decisions for you, including decisions about life support, in case you cannot make those decisions yourself
- Document II—The Washington Healthcare Directive, which lets you state your wishes about medical care in the event your attending physician determines that you have developed a terminal condition and can no longer make your own medical decisions.

The Washington Healthcare Directive also applies to conditions of permanent unconsciousness, like irreversible coma and persistent vegetative state. However, another doctor must agree with your attending physician's opinion.

The health care directive requires two adult witnesses. It is not valid in the case of pregnancy.

The durable power of attorney for health care does not require, but recommends, witnesses.

West Virginia: The West Virginia Advance Directive consists of three legal documents that protect your rights in medical treatments:

- The West Virginia Medical Power of Attorney lets you name someone to make decisions about your medical care, including decisions about life support, if you can no longer speak for yourself.
- The West Virginia Living Will lets you specify your wishes beforehand about your medical care in the event that you become terminally ill or enter a persistent vegetative state and can no longer make your own medical decisions. Your living will goes into effect when your doctor certifies in writing that you are terminally ill or in a persistent vegetative state.
- The West Virginia Combined Medical Power of Attorney and Living Will (optional) lets you name someone to make decisions about your medical care and specify your wishes ahead of time in the event you become terminally ill or enter a persistent vegetative state and can no longer make decisions about your medical care.

You have three options to complete these documents: to complete only a living will; only a medical power of attorney form; or the combined medical power of attorney form and the living will form.

In West Virginia the law states that your living will and the medical power of attorney require that you have two witnesses whose signatures, along with your signature, be made in front of a notary.

Wisconsin: The Wisconsin Advance Directive consists of two legal documents that protect your rights in medical decisions:

- The Wisconsin Power of Attorney for Healthcare lets you name someone to make decisions about your medical care—including decisions about life support if two physicians (or one physician and one psychologist) determine that you are unable to manage your own health care decisions.
- The Wisconsin Declaration to Physicians is your state's living will. It lets you state your wishes about the withholding or withdrawal of life-sustaining procedures or of feeding tubes in the event that you enter into a persistent vegetative state or develop a terminal illness. Although the declaration to physicians will be effective in most cases, it may not authorize the withholding or withdrawal of life-sustaining procedures or of feeding tubes if your attending physician determines that such withholding or withdrawal will cause you pain or discomfort.

The law requires that you date and sign your declaration to physicians and your power of attorney for health care in the presence of two adult witnesses, who must also sign the documents. These documents are not valid in the case of pregnancy. You do not have to have these documents notarized.

Wyoming: The Wyoming Advance Healthcare Directive is a legal document that protects your rights in medical decisions. It has four parts:
- The Wyoming Power of Attorney for Healthcare lets you name someone to make decisions about your health care—including decisions about life support—if you are no longer able to make your own decisions.
- The Wyoming Instructions for Healthcare functions as your state's living will. It lets you state ahead of time your wishes about health care in the event that you lack the capacity to make your own decisions, as determined by your primary physician or supervising physician.
- Donation of Organs at Death is an optional section that authorizes the donation of your organs at death.
- Primary Physician is an optional section that allows you to designate your primary physician as your health care provider.

The completed documents must either be signed before a notary public or, alternatively, witnessed by two adults.

CHAPTER FOUR
FEAR OF DYING AND DEATH

The fear of death is not a simple response with simple causes or answers. It has many components and is different for each of us. It is shaped by such factors as age and state of physical health; family, social, and religious backgrounds; and degree of psychological maturity. Our conscious fears may be little more than self-deceptions that cover up more accurate reactions to death. We will break the fears down into three categories: fear the process of dying; fear of the loss of life; and fear of what happens after death. Your task is to find out which of these fears apply to you. You may find yourself focusing on one of these categories, which seems to describe your kind of fear adequately; or you may find that your fear is composed of many elements; or you may find nothing really appropriate and be forced to consider other possibilities.

Much of what I say in this chapter may be graphically and emotionally difficult to read. What I am trying to do is not to be morbid, but merely offer stimulation to get you thinking about death and the dying process.

The Dying Process

Fear of the process of dying is much different from fear of what lies after death. As one person aptly put it, "I am afraid of dying rather than of death or being dead. . . . After it is all over I shall be beyond worrying, either in a state of eternal sleep, or some other state. . . . But, to be dying and to know it, how can I face it with tranquility?"

Some psychiatrists have observed this fear of the process of dying to be far more common than the fear of death itself, or of the afterlife. First there is the fear of pain. Most of us, if not all of us, see dying as being painful and physically agonizing, as well it can be. Fortunately, with modern medicine this is mostly an irrational fear, but not always. Modern drugs are not always effective.

The layperson tends to equate causes with pain, and to keep from having pain many people in our modern age request euthanasia or attempt suicide.

In the Christian tradition, it was thought that evil forces would be contesting for the soul of the departed, and the separation of the soul from the body was exceedingly painful.

There is also a fear of indignity. Some of us are actually ashamed to participate in dying. And these fears are very real. We do not always look our best as patients. The condition of our bed is embarrassing. Women may fear that they will not have their makeup on, or their hair combed, or may not have their dentures in. The room or the bedclothes may be very untidy. There may be a bedpan or medical paraphernalia connected to the person's body. There may be some intimate doings with the body which are thought not fit for public observation. There may well be an odor that bothers the patient, and hence he or she has a fear of visitors being bothered by it.

More than this, the disease may have ravaged the dying person's body or mind, or both. The patient may show uncharacteristic emotions. And the way some patients are treated by family members, or poorly trained hospital staff, increases their feeling of indignity. No, not all dying processes and deaths are dignified, to say the least; most are not.

Another fear that the dying person has, which probably trumps all other fears, is the fear of being a burden. There is no question that we will be a burden during the dying process, unless we just drop dead from a heart attack or something similar. Few of us will die this way, or by accident, and unfortunately, modern medicine prolongs our dying, often unnecessarily.

The dying patient may think of herself as being a burden to people who have to take care of her, or, if she is in the hospital, a burden to the people who come to visit. She may indeed become an emotional burden to others, which gives rise to all sorts of contradictory feelings among the family. She is the cause of strong feelings of empathy, sympathy, tenderness, and love; but there can also be feelings of disgust, pity, hate, and guilt. And, of course, the patient becomes a financial burden, especially if she is in a hospital or nursing home. It has been said that 90 percent of all doctor and prescription costs for a person come in the last few months of life. Seeing oneself as a burden during the dying process is certainly realistic.

Loss of Life

Now, rather than fear of what happens after death, or what happens during the process of dying, many of us fear death as the loss of life.

First, we have a fear of the loss of mastery. Most of us like to control things during our life. We desire to control ourselves, control others, and control our life's situations. We want to be active rather than passive, to participate in and change our present circumstances. We like to be in charge of at least our own destiny. And death spells the end of all our attempts to master.

We have a fear of incompleteness and failure. We love life supremely and cannot get enough of it. We want to live out completely all that is within us. This is to say we have ambitions. Men may want to finish out their vocational lives, and even after retirement they may want to be busy doing something for the betterment of the world.

Women may want to see their children raised and out on their own. They may want to be present at, and involved in, the birth and life of their grandchildren. Children want to at least get a good start on life. Yes, we have goals to reach, but death doesn't always respect them. We fear it because it destroys our relationships, our opportunities, our love, and everything we have known through the years we have been alive.

And finally, we fear death because it means separation. This is a most common and very complicated fear. We all express some sadness, and many of us have a real dread of being taken away from those we love. Many of us fear that our spouse or other loved ones can't manage without us. It is totally understandable that we grasp for the assurance that we will be united once again on the other side of death.

And, to me there definitely is the other side of death. In my ministry I have seen many examples of people talking to their loved ones on the other side as they were dying. But none of these were as striking as once when I was talking to a patient who was dying in the hospital. She was conversing with me and doing the talking when, all of a sudden, she said, "Oh, I have to go now, they are coming after me!" And she put her hands straight up in the air, and died. This was the most moving experience of my life. Since then, I have had no doubts that there is a hereafter.

This fear of separation is increased in our society by our reaction to the dying person. We are so overwhelmed by the impending disaster, and so afraid to speak of death to the dying, that our relationships are often destructive. Thus, the dying patient often realizes, correctly, that she is being abandoned. Three weeks before she died, one woman whom I counseled said, "My family has already given up. They have divorced themselves from me. They are even afraid to talk to me. If I could at least say goodbye to them, I would feel much better." In other words, the dying patient was more completely alone when she needed human contact the most.

Death separates, and our reaction to the dying increases that separation. It is no wonder that this specific fear is the most common of those I have described.

Family and friends should always recognize and be aware that there is a certain amount of fear involved with almost every dying patient. You should do your best to assuage these fears. The best way to do this is to be a good listener and let, and even encourage, the patient to vent his fears. Most patients will resist talking about their fears, but it is a good idea to give them permission to share them with you. Both of you will feel better afterward.

After Death

Most of us fear what happens to our body after death. The picture of a decaying body is not the most pleasant thing to think about. So we try embalming, purchase sturdy, leakproof caskets, and even have graves lined with metal or concrete. Some prefer cremations as an escape. Many of us refuse permission for autopsies, as we can't come to grips with what happens to the body. Many of us refuse to have our body parts used in medical education or transplanting into another person to keep them alive. We might refuse this even though intellectually we approve such practices. Emotionally we just can't accept it.

Most of us cannot picture our own bodies after we have died. We can visualize our funerals or memorial services, and the reactions of our loved ones and friends to our death, but it is too much to actually imagine our own corpse.

Many of us fear punishment. We know this fear has a long history, and it is understandable that anyone who has been raised to believe that there is a final judgment is likely to be concerned about it. Have I lived a good life? Have I been good? Have I helped my fellow man? Have I been a good husband, wife, father, mother? Will God accept me as I am? Will I go to heaven or hell? And so on. And we should not make the mistake of assuming that such fear does not occur in the minds of modern Christians who believe only in the saccharine heaven of a "nice guy" God. These Christians, too, have a fear of punishment after death—perhaps even more so.

Nor is the contemporary atheist or agnostic necessarily free from this fear. These long-standing and nearly universal beliefs in punishment would not have occurred without some basis in human experience, and this experience continues whether or not beliefs are clearly articulated. The fear of punishment has been around since the beginning of time.

Another great fear that most of us experience is the fear of the unknown. This is not always acknowledged as fear. As one person said, "I am not afraid of death . . . but there is a feeling which is akin to suspense . . . I have a feeling of insecurity." For some of us death is seen as Hamlet saw it, as an "undiscovered country, from whose bourn no traveller returns," and our response is at least uncertainty and often fear.

It may well be that the fear of punishment may increase in our generation, as the charts of the afterlife, so carefully detailed by traditional beliefs, tend to fade away.

When I speak of the fear of dying and death, I am always reminded of the great quote by Socrates when a group of his followers tried to persuade him to flee into exile after he was condemned to die by the rulers of Athens.

Socrates was a philosopher, and he was only interested in philosophizing about human problems. His guiding rule was "Know thyself." He believed that goodness in a man was based on wisdom, and wickedness was based on ignorance. No wise man would deliberately choose what was bad for him in the long run, but most men, through ignorance, may choose an evil that appears to be good at the time.

Socrates was always loyal to the democratic form of government in Athens. During the reign of terror that followed the death of Pericles, he disobeyed the order of the Thirty Tyrants to bring in a fellow citizen for execution and therefore was sentenced to death. It was then that he pronounced his famous quote:

> *To fear death, gentlemen, is nothing else than to think*
> *one is wise when one is not; for it is thinking one knows*
> *what one does not know. For no one knows whether death*
> *be not even the greatest of all blessings to man, but they*
> *fear it as if they knew that it is the greatest of evils. And*
> *is not this the most reprehensible form of ignorance, that*
> *of thinking one knows what one does not know?*

With that, the great philosopher raises the cup of hemlock, brought to him by his jailer, to his lips. He makes a toast to the gods and drinks the bitter poison. He met death with the same calm and self-control with which he had lived.

Almost all other cultures have regarded death as the ultimate friend. They knew that generations pass. In our culture, we try to make believe this is not so.

CHAPTER FIVE

SHOULD THE PATIENT BE TOLD?
SHOULD SCIENCE PROLONG LIFE?

In our contemporary society, we find emphasis placed on youth, health, and beauty, as if this is the epitome of life. Early retirement plans make room for youth to take over increasingly in business and industry. Special villages for the retired and the aging are set up apart from the rest of society, as if to say, "If you must get old and die, please go off somewhere by yourselves and do it."

At the same time that we venerate youth, medical advances lengthen life, and a growing percentage of the population is of advanced years.

A century ago, nearly every family had representatives of two or three generations in it. The young and old shared a common roof and a common bond, and there was a healthy interchange of philosophy and experience.

Today the effort to separate generations, with a premium on youth, creates false values and denies reality. In effect it tries to say that aging and dying are not to be considered a part of life.

The truth is, however, that everybody is a terminal case—all of us at one time or another must face death. Therefore, we must look at everyone as a dying person, regardless of age.

While death is experienced all around us, we build up walls against the healthful discussion of its meanings for persons and society. The dying patient, living in this unreal and prohibitive atmosphere, is caught in the social restraint that makes his need greater at the same time that the opportunity to satisfy it is made increasingly difficult. This separates him from the normal communications of family and community by a conspiracy of silence.

People live on meaning, and any act or attitude that fails to share the quest for meaning, even in the tragic events such as death, is a denial of relationships that cannot easily be accepted. The goals of those in relationship with the terminal patient are to strengthen the meaning of life, for this may very well restore life.

Help, then, is really needed in terms of how to live, not how to die. Man's ultimate challenge in dying, then, is to determine if it has meaning , or is it the ultimate in meaninglessness. In pain, a person can endure much more if life has meaning to him. The quest for meaning, therefore, gives to pain and death a direction and a purpose. Likewise, one way to reduce a patient's fear of death is to rearouse his creative impulses. The great philosopher Carl Jung said, "There is a need of the person to find meaning for his dying, just as he sought meaning for his living." For those of us who are around the dying patient, our role is not merely that of bringing peace, but also meaning and order to the events that are being experienced. One should try to give meaning to death in accord with the person's meaning to life, so that the act of dying is not separated from life but is rather a continuation of the mood and manner of living.

However, one thing to always keep in mind is you should never give false hope. The concentration should be more on the expansion and feeling of the self rather than on physical recovery.

So now we get to the heart of the chapter: should the dying person be told of his condition? This question continues to be a controversial subject, but in view of what has been said previously, it is quite evident, I'm sure, that I firmly believe the patient should be told—to be sure, at the right time and in the proper way. I believe we have no right to withhold such information from the person involved. This, of course, is not always the easiest road to follow, but it is the road that can lead to very fruitful encounters and a sense of community in the life of the patient.

A case in point: When I was living in Maine, I believe it was in 1972, I read an article in the newspaper about a forty-two-year-old man who was told, quite bluntly by the doctor, that he had only a year to live. He related the tremendous shock that came over him and his wife. He went through every stage of the "stages of dying," but in the end he accepted his fate and resolved to live each day to its fullest extent. In his words: "I made up my mind to live one day at a time, enjoying life to its fullest, and soon I was doing just that. A wonderful and understanding wife and children made it possible. Christmas was our best ever, lot of laughing, good food, meeting friends, gifts. That night I had a good cry when the kids were in bed and I was alone. It was my last Christmas with my family. I cried hard and I am not ashamed to say so. In January I felt pretty good and Bev and I flew to Jamaica for a week of fun in the sun."

If this man had not been told of his impending death, perhaps he would not have been able to live out his life to its fullest, or able to "set his house in order."

In my forty years of ministry I have experienced many such events. People have told me that they never lived until they were told they had a terminal disease. After being told, they said every moment they were alive meant everything to them. Each day was a special gift, and they lived each moment to the fullest. This pretty well proves the statement, "You will never truly live until you come to grips with your own death."

I have found that most terminal patients are well aware of their condition before being told by the doctor, and not telling them makes it necessary for them to use up their energy in "protecting their family" from the truth.

When our daughter died we were told the truth about her illness almost as soon as the doctor knew, and I suspect this is true in most cases when one's child is terminally ill. Often little effort is made to prepare parents for such dreadful news. One wonders if there exists an assumption among doctors that parents can cope with the truth about their children more easily than they can with truth about themselves.

The terminally ill patient often has an unconscious fear of being "untouchable," and it is very difficult for her to have a healthy attitude toward dying when those around her are saturated with unhealthy feelings toward her. Thus the feelings expressed by Robert Frost seem all too true: *"No, from the time one is sick unto death, one is alone."*

Because of this taboo, the experience of dying can be cruelly isolating, with no one daring to broach the subject to the dying person, and his uneasy awareness that for him to bring it up would be to invite further isolation.

This point is made in vivid detail by Tolstoy in *The Death of Ivan Ilyich.* What tormented Ivan Ilyich the most was the deception shown by his family and friends. They were not willing to admit what they all knew, as he also knew, so they lied to him and forced him to participate in that lie. He had thus to live all alone on the brink of an abyss, with no one who understood or pitied him.

Unfortunately, so often we send the dying patient to an impersonal hospital room with disinterested people around him, at the time when he most needs the comfort and support of his familiar surroundings and the members of his family. If the family can be helped to take a healthy view of death and dying, they can stand in close relationship with the dying patient. This may not involve many words. Often the patient, without saying a word, will open his eyes and look around the room, or feel the touch of a hand upon his and will know that in the lonely pilgrimage into death, those who love him have not deserted him in their fears but are standing by him in their desire to share his life to the end. A feeling of community, shared emotions, and an honest facing of reality seem to undergird life with strength rather than shatter it with weakness.

Dying persons often, toward the end, give a strenuous effort both on the conscious level and the unconscious level to bring order and meaning into life, as if to end things in a neat and tidy manner. This is why many times we see dying patients seem to rejuvenate, rally, and feel much better just before they die.

However, it is a feeling of guilt, more than anything else, that separates a dying person from those around him, as well as from his God. Much of this guilt stems from the patient's belief that his illness is a sign of sin, and death a form of punishment. Our role in ministering to the dying is to assure him that this view is not supported by the New Testament teaching, and it violates the whole concept of medical practice. If illness were a form of punishment, then the physician would be guilty of meddling in matters of divine judgment. If death were the final form of punishment, then there would be evidence of an indiscriminate judge at work, for all that lives, dies, so the logic of the premise is undermined.

The person dying in faith and devotion with his family and community performs a most meaningful emotional service. To die in faith is a witness of God's love, which brings courage and hope to the whole community.

Should We Prolong a Person's Life Artificially?

Trained to regard death as the enemy they must defeat at all costs, some doctors regularly resort to heroic measures to keep their patients alive. They are, after all, trained to heal and keep people alive. Fortunately times are changing, and doctors recently out of medical school have a different outlook. But there still remain many who will resort to radical surgery or use complex machines to maintain a flicker of life in people so old and ravaged as to be beyond caring.

But does death always represent defeat? "No," says Dr. William Poe, a professor of community medicine at Duke University. Poe, whose father was a Baptist minister, says, "I am pretty well steeped in the Golden Rule, and I am old enough to figure how I'd want to be treated someday. I don't want to be cycled and recycled to the doctor, to the specialist, to the hospital. I am against the hauling and mauling of people who have no reasonable future."

Poe does not advocate euthanasia. "We are not supposed to shorten life," he says. "But there is a limit to what we ought to do to prolong it."

To prepare for my doctoral dissertation I organized a *Thanatos* group in which I worked with six doctors and a psychiatrist. We would meet at least once a week, or on call, to go over several patients' charts and history to advocate the proper treatment, or no treatment, whichever the particular case called for. Many times we would come to a unanimous decision that we should keep the patient as comfortable as possible, but withhold any treatment that would prolong life. I would often remark, "Are we prolonging the life of the patient, or are we prolonging the dying process?" "Is the person really alive who must remain under sedation all of the time?" "When does a person really die? When the heart stops beating? When the mind stops functioning? When he is no longer a personality?" I firmly believed, and still do, that these are questions that must be asked. I also believe quality of life is much more important than length of life. I was scheduled to do this project for a year, but when the year was up, the doctors, to a person, said, "No way are we going to stop these meetings." They were very pleased with the outcome of the meetings. I was considered a colleague and a very important cog in the group. We kept meeting until I moved out of town many years later. Parenthetically, they were always happy to see me come down the hall in the hospital after one of their patients died. Then they could turn the grieving family over to me for comfort. Most doctors I have known have a difficult time dealing with a grieving family.

I have also known many doctors who have come down with cancer of one type or another, and the largest percentage of them will not take chemotherapy or even radiation if the outlook is not favorable. They usually say, "Let nature take its course; sometimes the treatment is much worse than the illness."

Dr. Elisabeth Kübler-Ross observed: "Dying nowadays is more gruesome in many ways. It is lonelier, more mechanical, and more dehumanized." Actually, in many ways, we are more humane to our animals than we are to our fellow human beings. When an animal becomes terminally ill, we have it put away—euthanized. When a person becomes terminally ill, we keep him alive as long as possible and in so doing prolong his suffering needlessly.

I could site many cases in which I have been involved where I believe there has been malpractice by the physician. A case in point: a parishioner, Charlie, was diagnosed with bone cancer. He was given two months to live. He had trouble with his legs one day and was taken to the hospital, where a doctor examined him and said he had gangrene in the leg and it would have to be amputated. I happened to call on him shortly after the diagnosis, and he told me what the doctor had said to him. I said, "Charlie, do you want that to be done?" He said, "I sure don't, but what am I going to do, the doctor says it has to be done." His wife was sitting in the room, and I asked her what she thought. She also said she thought it was ridiculous, taking into account that he had just been given two months to live because of bone cancer. I asked the couple if they would give me permission to intercede for them, and they said, certainly. I called the doctor and told him what they said and what they didn't want done. He said, "Dr. Laramy, do you know how painful gangrene can be?" I said, "No, I don't. But I do know how painful bone cancer can be, and if the gangrene takes his life sooner, it will probably be a blessing." I am sure the doctor could see a malpractice suit in the future, so he declined to do the amputation. Charlie lived for less than two months, but what he had left of his life he lived to the fullest, and he and his wife thanked me profusely for interceding for them. As I said, this is just one case of many in which I interceded for the patient, but I was glad to do it, and glad they gave me permission to stop a foolish and meaningless procedure.

I firmly believe in the statement of Dr. Roland Stevens, a surgeon who champions the Death-With-Dignity cause at the University of Rochester Medical School:

"A doctor must learn that humane considerations sometimes supersede scientific techniques."

I personally believe that those who have terminal cancer, or whose brain is irreversibly damaged, or who will only live as more vegetable than human, have the right to die peacefully. They should get palliative care, good food and liquids, and, if possible, be kept comfortable and be allowed to die peacefully and with dignity.

CHAPTER SIX
THE DYING PROCESS

Let me not pray to be sheltered from
dangers but to be fearless in facing them.
Let me not beg for the stilling of my pain
but for the heart to conquer it.
Let me not look for allies in life's
battlefield but to my own strength.
Let me not crave in anxious fear
to be saved but hope for the patience
to win my freedom.
Grant me that I may not be a coward,
feeling your mercy in my success alone;
but let me find the grasp of your hand in my future.
Rabindranath Tagore

Now that we have covered all the things necessary to get ready for the dying process, I would like to share some things I have learned through these many years of ministry, as far as the dying process is concerned, and hopefully help people to understand what is happening, what to expect, and some ways to cope with the final stages of our growth.

The most famous name in bringing death "out of the closet" so we can look at it, and talk about it, was Dr. Elisabeth Kübler-Ross, who wrote *On Death and Dying*, published in 1969. I had the privilege and honor of studying "at the feet" of this great scholar. I would like to pass on to my readers some of the insights, as far as death and dying is concerned, that she passed on to me.

To begin with, let's be honest: none of us really wants to talk about this subject. Yet we have sometimes been defined as the only creatures who know, at least intellectually, that we will die. Emotionally is another thing entirely. Because we are thinking individuals, we are able to evade, deny, or repress the knowledge of our death. However, only as we come to grips with the reality of death for ourselves, as well as for others, do we find the freedom to really live. In other words, if we exist with the dark cloud of death constantly hanging over our heads, we cannot live life to its fullest.

Many observers of our contemporary American society see a nation or culture hiding from the realities of death. Not too many years ago—perhaps in the lifetime of many who are reading this book—when someone was dying, everyone in the neighborhood knew about it, even to the youngest child.

The dying person remained in his home and was surrounded by family and friends through the whole ordeal. At the moment of death, these people would be at his bedside, holding his hands, caressing his forehead. They would hear from and speak last words to the dying person. They would see the cessation of breathing, relaxation of the body, and the loss of skin color. Members of the family would bathe and prepare the body for last rites. Many, if not all, of the people in the community would attend these rites. There would be no escaping the consciousness of death. Everyone would see the reality of life and death. This, to me, is a very healthy and normal procedure.

Today, unfortunately, we are not as likely to die at home with friends gathered around us, as among strangers in a hospital or nursing home. We are not likely to sip soup in our own bed, but rather to be fed intravenously or through an external food tube. Instead of saying farewell to family and friends, we are more likely to be surrounded by a conspiracy of silence and pretense. No matter at what age we die, the final moments of life will rarely be observed by our families.

And yet we see stirrings and signs that the new generation has a new attitude toward dying. We live in a day when the subject of "dying with dignity" has once again come to the forefront of our thinking. Unfortunately, however, the very triumphs of medicine and technology that have conquered so much disease in America have also spawned resuscitators, tubes, machines, and intravenous feedings, which are able to keep us alive long after, on our own, we would have died. We are beginning to learn that life at any cost is not necessarily a bargain, that heroic measures to keep the organism going may virtually destroy the quality of life and relationships. This is why it is so important to make our wishes known through a living will and a medical power of attorney.

No one has done more to sensitize us to the needs of dying people than Dr. Kübler-Ross. She was a pioneer in interviewing patients in a seminar setting for the benefit of future physicians, nurses, and pastors as to the patient's needs and desires. Out of her experiences and conversations, Kübler-Ross listed five stages that many, if not most, dying patients go through. We will discuss these in order to get a sense of the needs of both the terminally ill patients and their families and loved ones.

The first stage is **denial**. This is the, "No, not me," stage. A classic, if humorous, example of the denial stage is the statement a man once made to his wife: "If one of us dies, I'm going to Paris."

First of all we must acknowledge the fact that dying is a part of life. This is very hard to do in this youth-minded society in which we live. We live in a society that denies death. Once a person dies, the cosmetician applies makeup so the dead person still looks very much alive and youthful, sometimes even more so than in his last days, and we say, "Doesn't he look natural!"

Even at the cemetery the groundskeepers lay a green cover over the hole that has been dug to camouflage the fact that the casket is indeed going to be buried in the ground. Then the funeral director ushers the people back to their cars so they won't see the actual lowering of the casket. All of this is a denial that a death has taken place.

We try to ignore death completely, if possible, and if it isn't, we deny its harshness. You don't believe me? Let's look at some more facts.

We do not die anymore, we pass away, we go to sleep, we expire, we depart, we pass on, etc. We don't fill out a death certificate, but rather we fill out a "vital statistics form." We are advised not to buy a burial plot, but rather we "invest in a pre-need memorial estate." We have even changed the words in the marriage ceremony from "until death do us part" to "as long as we both shall live." Our language and actions at the occasion of death indicate our need to deny its harshness. To me this is unhealthy, as we have a hard time coming to grips with the fact that our loved one is, in fact, gone.

There is still another way we deny death, and it is more subtle than either ignoring death completely or denying its harshness. Our society seems to be preoccupied with death. The newspapers, comic books, westerns, detective stories, many spy novels, and horror movies achieve mass circulation by the very inclusion of numerous and detailed presentations of violent death. Why?

According to social anthropologist Geoffrey Gorer, our fascination is pornographic. These presentations of dying and death make little room for our normal feelings of sorrow, guilt, and love. The creators of James Bond , and many others, seem only to be making each successive novel contain more spectacular ways of dying. Therefore, death, like sex, is depersonalized and sensationalized as a way of avoiding its reality in human life. In other words, we deny death by means of morbid preoccupation with bizarre fantasies.

The three most likely professions to be represented at the time a person is dying are doctors, nurses, and members of the clergy. Unfortunately we see a tremendous tendency in these professions to also deny the reality of death. They deny it behind a shield of objectivity. If they can disassociate from the dying, keep from identifying with him, withdraw from him emotionally, they then can depersonalize him, regard him as an object, and safely handle him as a thing.

If he is no longer a person like ourselves, he cannot touch us, clutch onto us, drag us down with him. "It's a sad case," says the doctor. "It's terminal," says the nurse. "Poor thing," says the minister.

Ritual is also a shield for the professional. The ritual of the doctor consists of following the entire last-ditch rubrics in the book as he pronounces the patient dead. The ritual of the nurse is regulating oxygen, an IV drip, taking blood pressure, counting pulse and respiration until there is none. The ritual of the clergyperson consists of hearing confession, reading scripture, and saying prayers.

Doctrine is also a shield. No one knows what death is really like, and yet we have to explain it somehow, lest we be forced to admit we do not know and find ourselves faced with a void. We all use doctrine to help explain it—the doctor, "in terms of the cause of death" and a final note of summary on the patient's chart; the nurse, in recording the diminishing vital signs and registering the circumstances of the dying, step by step; the clergyperson, with words about the "will of God" and "life hereafter."

Even the hospitals are prone to denial of death. They almost always will put a dying patient at the end of the hall so they don't have to look in on him so often and be reminded that he is dying. This may not be done intentionally, but in more cases than not, this is what happens.

So we protect ourselves from the threat of death and against the unknowable by ignoring it altogether, denying its harshness, sensationalizing it, or in the case of professionals, by doctrine, ritual, and objectivity.

So, in conclusion, we all are guilty of denying death, and that's all right, as long as we are aware of the fact that that is what we are doing. If we don't come to grips with this fact, it can lead to what we call morbid grief, which I will discuss in another chapter.

Sigmund Freud concluded:

Our own death is indeed unimaginable, and whenever we make an attempt to imagine it we can perceive that we really survive as spectators. Hence, the psychoanalytic school could venture the assertion that at the bottom line, no one believes in his own death, or, to put the same thing in another way, in the unconscious, every one of us is convinced of his own immortality.

The second stage of dying is **anger**. "Why me?" may be the patient's hostile question. "I have lived a good, clean life!" "I haven't hurt anyone!" "I have tried to help others!" "I go to church every Sunday!" "Why me?"

This anger is natural and to be expected. Life is being cut off, and the patient becomes envious of those alive and well around him. Even the family may be received at this time with less than a warm welcome.

The doctors, nurses, clergyperson, and family must not take this anger personally. He is not railing out at you, he is railing at what is taking place within his body, and it is vented to you, as a means of getting rid of his emotions. If you begin to withdraw from the patient's anger, you will tend to isolate him, and he will become angrier and lonelier. A patient who is listened to and respected regardless of his anger will soon settle down and lower his voice, because he is being taken seriously.

The family may also be experiencing lots of anger. They, too, may rail at the doctor, nurses, and clergy. Can you blame them? Their loved one is being taken from them. They are facing a tremendous void in their lives. The family may also experience anger at the dying patient because he is leaving them and putting them through such an ordeal.

Another caution: we often focus so much of our attention upon the dying person that we neglect other members of the family who are weary, tired, frustrated, and emotionally drained.

Because in crisis we often tend to revert to the magical thinking of childhood, and because we all have mixed feelings toward the important people in our lives, we may be troubled with the thought that our anger has somehow contributed to the patient's sickness. In other words, we blame ourselves for what's happening, and then we have tremendous guilt feelings. This is often the case with young children. These reactions are perfectly normal when there is a dying loved one in our midst.

The third stage of dying is **bargaining**. This stage is not as well known, but it is equally helpful to the patient, though usually for a very short time. We consciously make some sort of agreement that will postpone the inevitable. We have used denial and anger and they haven't done any good, so we resort to bargaining. We become very much like a child when he doesn't get his own way. He will get angry, then he will try to bargain: "If I am good for a week and help you around the house, will you let me?" In the case of the dying person, she almost always will bargain for more time, followed by a wish for a few more days without pain or physical discomfort. It is really an attempt to postpone the inevitable, but it has to include a prize offered "for good behavior." It also sets a self-imposed "deadline" and includes an implicit promise that the patient will not ask for more if this one postponement is granted. Of course, most patients will not keep their promise. As an example, Helen bargains with God, "If you will let me live until my son graduates from college, I will be ready to go." However, when she does attend her son's graduation, she comes back to the bargaining table and says, "Remember, God, I still have another son!" It is like saying, "If I can have one more dish of ice cream, then I will go on my diet." I have found that most bargaining is done with God and is usually kept a secret or shared with the pastor. A number of patients will promise a life dedicated to God or a life dedicated to the church in exchange for some additional time. Psychologically, promises may be associated with feelings of guilt. Therefore, it would behoove the pastor to not brush away these remarks. The patient may feel guilty that she didn't do as much as she could have in different areas—didn't teach Sunday school, participate in the choir, be a deaconess, attend services often enough, and so on. The person should be helped to be relieved of these irrational feelings of guilt. She should be helped in her quest to accept forgiveness, or to be relieved of the need for self-punishment.

The fourth stage of dying is **depression**. When the terminally ill patient can no longer deny her illness, when she is forced to undergo more surgery, chemotherapy, radiation, then she cannot smile, bargain, wish it off anymore. Then her numbness or stoicism, the anger and rage, will soon be replaced with a great sense of loss. She will begin to think about the tremendous expenses, loss of home, loss of family, and burdens of all kinds, which will all add to her sadness and guilt. This, my friends, is called depression! The psychological definition of depression is anger turned inward.

There are two kinds of depression that affect the terminally ill: reactive depression and preparatory depression. They differ tremendously in nature and should be dealt with quite differently.

Reactive depression usually takes place with past loss—for example, a woman having to have breast removal because of cancer. She can be helped to overcome depression by accentuating other features. She can be cheered up, and the patient herself can add many things to the conversation.

Preparatory depression usually takes place with impending loss of life. This patient cannot be cheered up, nor does he want to be. The patient should not be encouraged to look at the sunny side of things. This would mean he should not contemplate his impending death. In other words, it would only tend to reinforce his denial.

On the other hand, if the patient is allowed to express his sorrow, he will find a final acceptance much easier, and he will be grateful to those who can sit with him during this stage of depression without being judgmental or constantly telling him that he shouldn't be so sad and down.

In contrast to reactive depression, preparatory depression is usually a silent type of depression. There is usually no or little need for words. It is usually more a feeling that can be expressed much better by holding hands, giving a hug, stroking one's forehead, or just plain sitting together without conversation. I personally have sat by a bedside for twenty-four hours holding a dying patient's hand with hardly a word being spoken. He was waiting for his son to arrive from out of town. He would drop off to sleep and then wake up saying, "Oh, you're still here with me; that's good," and then drop off to sleep once again. His son finally appeared the next day, had time with his father, and the father died a few hours later.

Preparatory depression is necessary and beneficial if the patient is to die in a stage of acceptance and peace. Only patients who have been able to work through their anguish and anxieties are able to achieve this stage. If this reassurance can be shared with the family and loved ones, they, too, can be spared much unnecessary anguish.

The fifth and last stage of dying is **acceptance**. If the patient has been given the help and understanding through the previously described stages, he will finally reach the stage of acceptance. This is the stage during which he is neither depressed nor angry about his impending death. He will have been able to express his previous feelings, his envy for the living and the healthy, his anger at those who do not have to face death so soon. He will have mourned the impending loss of so many meaningful people and places, and he will contemplate his coming end of life with a certain degree of quiet expectation.

He will usually be quite tired and, in most cases, weak. He will doze off quite often, but it will be a peaceful sleep, rather than the fitful rest during the times of depression. It is a gradual increasing need to extend the hours of sleep, very similar to the pattern of a newborn child, but in reverse order. Fortunately, in most cases, it is not a resigned and hopeless "giving up" sense of "what's the use?" or "I just can't fight it any longer." Rather it is a time of peace and tranquillity.

The acceptance stage is the time when the loved ones of the patient should discourage other people's visits, as they will usually try to cheer up the patient and hinder his emotional preparation for death rather than enhance it.

At the same time, however, acceptance should not be mistaken for a happy stage. It is a time of almost a void of any feelings. It is as if all the pain is gone, the struggle is over, and the time for final rest has come.

It is at this time that the family and loved ones usually need more help and understanding, support and comfort, than the patient himself.

While the dying patient has found some peace and acceptance, his circle of interest diminishes drastically. He wishes to be left alone or at least not stirred up by news and problems of the outside world. This is definitely not the time to talk politics or about pending trips, cruises, or even about future family affairs. Again, visitors are often not desired, and if they do come, the patient is no longer in a talkative mood. He often requests limits on the number of people in the room and prefers short visits. This is the time the TV is off, and communication becomes more nonverbal than verbal. He may often just make gestures of the hand to invite the visitor to sit down for a while. He may just hold the hand of the visitor and ask him to sit in silence. Such moments of silence may be the most meaningful communications for people who are not uncomfortable in the presence of a dying person. The visitor may just let the patient know that it is all right to say nothing after the usual greetings upon arrival.

A visit in the evening usually lends itself to a very meaningful encounter, as it is the end of the day both for the visitor and the patient. If the patient is in the hospital, it is the time when the hospital's page system does not interrupt such a moment, when the nurse does not come in to take the vitals, and the cleaning woman is not mopping the floor.

It takes such a little time for the visit, but it is comforting to the patient to know that he has not been forgotten when nothing else can be done for him. It is gratifying for the visitor as well, for it will show him or her that dying is not such a frightening, horrible thing that so many want to avoid. One thing to remember is that none of us gets out of this life alive. And by visiting the dying patient, this becomes very real to the visitor.

How, then, do we know when a patient is giving up "too early," when a little more fight on his part, in our opinion, combined with the help of the medical profession, could give him a chance to live a little longer? How can we differentiate this from the stage of acceptance, when our wish to prolong life often contradicts his wish to rest and die in peace?

When we are unable to differentiate these two stages, we do more harm than good to the patient; we will be frustrated in our efforts, and make his dying a painful last experience.

Patients who are in the stage of acceptance show a very outstanding feeling of equanimity and peace. There is something very dignified with these patients, while people in a state of resignation are very often indignant, full of bitterness and anguish, and very often express the statements "What's the use?" or "I'm tired of fighting!" It is a feeling of futility, or uselessness and lack of peace, which is quite easily distinguishable from the genuine stage of acceptance.

One last statement regarding the acceptance stage: by all means, don't forget the family of the dying patient; at this stage they are hurting more than the dying patient and need your help, prayers, and comfort!

Having said all of this about "stages of dying," one thing must be very clear: a person can move from one stage to the other and then back again—for example, from acceptance all the way back to denial, or to bargaining, and so on. Nothing in the stages of dying is "set in concrete," and everyone is different in how he or she handles it.

I recently lost my younger brother, Dick. I had the fortunate opportunity to spend five weeks with him before he died. Frankly, aside from bargaining and acceptance, I did not see much evidence of any of the other stages I have just mentioned. However, a person never knows what is going through the mind of another person. I asked him point-blank what his feelings were about dying. He said, "I don't fear death, but I do fear the dying process. I would like to stick around until after the election, because I am curious to see how that pans out." (*Bargaining*). "I certainly do not want to leave Marilyn and the kids, as I love them very much, but, as you know, I have loved ones on the other side, too, and I am sort of anxious to see them once again." Dick seemed to reach the acceptance stage very quickly and did not go back to any of the other stages to any extent. I definitely noticed toward the end that he really did not want to converse very much. He slept a lot, and was happy to just have someone hold his hand and sit with him. If he was in any pain he certainly didn't show it, and if asked, he would say no. The workers at hospice, which I will talk about in a later chapter, were absolutely marvelous. They were so attentive and ready to help in any way they could, no matter what time of day or night.

CHAPTER SEVEN
RIGHTS AND NEEDS OF THE DYING PATIENT

I would like to list some of the rights and needs of the dying patient as I have observed and formulated them over many years in the ministry:

Rights
- To be heard
- To be told the facts
- To share in the decision making, including the right to refuse treatment
- To be told if his condition is terminal
- To die when his body and spirit are ready
- To be cared for by physicians with a positive attitude toward palliative care

Physiological Needs
- The patient's sensation and power of motion as well as his reflexes are lost in the legs first and gradually in the arms:
  1. Pressure on the extremities bothers the patient.
  2. The skin is sore to the touch.
  3. The sheets should not be snug around the patient.
  4. The patient should be turned frequently to avoid bedsores. Pay particular attention to the position of the legs, because as the dying process advances, the patient has very little control and strength to move his legs.
- As peripheral circulation fails, there usually is a drenching sweat, and the body surface cools, regardless of room temperature.

1. The patient is not conscious of being cold regardless of how cold the body surface feels to touch.
2. Restlessness is often caused by sensation of heat.
   Tossing about is the patient's attempt to throw off the bedcovers.
3. An oxygen tent usually will not help, unless the patient is having trouble breathing.

- The dying patient will almost always face the light
  1. Try to have indirect lighting in the room.
  2. Never draw the shades.
  3. Never turn out the light at night.
  4. Never whisper in the corner of the room. Remember that a person's hearing is the last thing to go, and he will think you are talking about him, even though you may not be.
  5. Never fail to answer the patient's questions honestly.
  6. The patient's touch may be diminished, yet he can usually sense pressure. Always try to find out if the patient wants to be touched, as touch can be an intrusion, and skin can be extremely tender. Watch for nonverbal signals. If the patient pulls away from your touch, it is for a reason. Sometimes he will not let you know the reason, as he does not want to offend you.
  7. The patient may seem in terrible pain throughout the dying process but usually isn't toward the end.
  8. Be sure to treat the patient as a person until the end. Again, remember that hearing usually is the last sense to go, so don't hesitate to talk to the patient, even though he or she does not respond.

Psychological Needs

- Pain can be very real, but it can also be psychological. Assure the patient that everything is being done that can be done.
- The patient can have a feeling of acute loneliness. This has a profound relationship to pain. Pain is almost always more severe when the patient is left alone, so it is best to make sure someone is with the patient at all times—even if it is only sitting in a chair in the patient's room.
- Be very sensitive to the urgent plea—either verbal or nonverbal—"Please don't leave me alone." This can be either symbolic or direct.
- With older people, loneliness can be expressed by hostility. Always remember that the hostility is not directed at you; it is directed at what is taking place with the patient herself. She is angry at the very fact that she is dying, and nothing can be done about it.

Spiritual Needs

- The patient should be made to feel that she is important at all times.
- The patient needs to be affirmed.
- The patient needs to be assured that God has not forsaken her or left her in her time of need, that God is still very much with her through her trials.
- The patient may want you to pray with her. If you are uncomfortable doing that, call her minister or the chaplain in the hospital or hospice.
- The patient may want you to read scripture. Most hospital rooms have a Gideon Bible in the patient's bedside stand.
- Always respect the patient's feelings of belief, or unbelief. This certainly is not a time for proselytizing.
- The most important thing to do is LISTEN!
- Be aware and alert to religious guilt feelings; let the patient ventilate without being judgmental. Try not to share what you think about the situation, unless the patient asks you.
- Don't be afraid to cry and feel with and for the patient, but only to the extent that you do not become part of the problem instead of part of the solution.

Helping the Family of the Dying Patient

- If you are a visitor and are not a member of the family, you can be of considerable support to the family.
- First and foremost, be a good listener to both the patient and the family.
- Always be aware of nonverbal as well as verbal signals.
- Let the family take care of the patient, unless they ask you to help.
- Do not condone, or be involved in, indiscriminate bedside comments. If there are other visitors present, do not start a conversation that will not include the dying patient and her family. Always be aware of the patient and try not to stray from including her in your conversation.
- By all means do not prejudge the family. They are going through a very difficult time and may say things that to you are "off the wall," but remember that anything they do or say at a time like this may be perfectly normal, even if it doesn't seem that way to you.
- Feel free to express your emotions, as long as it doesn't interfere and become embarrassing to the dying patient or her family.

CHAPTER EIGHT
HOSPICE

You matter because of who you are. You matter to the last moment of your life, and we will do all we can, not only to help you die peacefully, but also to help you live until you die. Dame Cicely Saunders

Hospice, in the early days, was a concept rooted in the centuries-old idea of offering a place of shelter and rest, or hospitality to weary and sick travelers on a long journey. In 1967 Dame Cicely Saunders at St. Christopher's Hospice in London first applied the term "hospice" to specialized care for dying patients.

I was fortunate to be a table monitor at a workshop at St. Christopher's Hospital in Montreal, Canada, in the 1970s at which Dame Cicely Saunders and Dr. Elisabeth Kübler-Ross were presenters. It was an honor for me to be in the presence of these two giants who have taken death out of the closet so we can speak openly about it. I also felt good because I was instrumental in bringing the hospice movement to International Falls, Minnesota, and subsequently to Sun City, Arizona.

As I have mentioned before, however, the hospice movement never meant so much to me as it did while my brother was dying last year. The hospice volunteers and professionals were absolutely great and did so much to help my sister-in-law, her family, my wife, and me through this very difficult time in our lives.

Today, hospice provides humane and compassionate care for tens of thousands of people in the last phases of incurable disease so they may live as fully and comfortably as possible.

Hospice is a philosophy of care that accepts death as the final stage of life. Its goal is to enable patients to continue an alert, pain-free life if possible and to manage other symptoms so that their last days may be spent with dignity and quality, surrounded by their loved ones. It is important to note that hospice affirms life and does not hasten or postpone death. Hospice treats the person rather than the disease. It provides family-centered care and involves the patient and the family in making decisions. Care is provided for the patient and the family twenty-four hours a day, seven days a week. When my brother died at two o'clock in the morning, we called hospice, and a nurse was there within fifteen minutes. All of the personnel in that particular hospice were just wonderful.

Hospice care can be given in the home, nursing home, hospital, or in a free-standing hospice unit. Most hospice care in the United States is given in the home of the patient, with the family being the main caregivers.

In my experience I have found that hospices run by hospitals are, for the most part, not as successful, or as caring, as free-standing hospices. The reason, perhaps, is that hospitals are for treating and healing patients and are not geared for palliative care. This is not to say that some are not exceptionally good at palliative care. Again In my experience, hospital hospices run by Catholic nuns are exceptional.

Care begins when you are admitted to the program, which generally means that a hospice team member visits the home to learn about your situation and needs. Return visits are set up so that your needs can be reevaluated regularly. To handle around-the-clock patient needs or crises, home hospice programs have an on-call nurse who answers phone calls day and night, makes home visits, or sends the appropriate team member, if needed, between scheduled visits. Medicare-certified hospices are required to provide nursing, pharmacy, and doctor services around the clock.

Hospice care is recommended when patients no longer benefit from treatment for their terminal disease, and their life expectancy is six months or less. Hospice helps the patient really live until she dies. Hospice does not in any way strive for cure.

One of the problems with hospice care is that, in many cases, it is not started in time. The average time in hospice is quite often only a few days, or weeks at the most. Unfortunately, sometimes the patient, the doctor, or the family looks at hospice as giving up hope. This is not true, because if you get better or your disease goes into remission, you can be taken out of the hospice program and go back to hospice care at a later time, if needed. The hope that hospice brings is the hope of quality life, making the best of each day during the last stages of an advanced illness.

Most hospices have an interdisciplinary group of people, all striving to make the patient's last days as free of pain as possible, as well as meaningful. Most hospices have trained volunteers, nurses on staff, and doctors on staff or on call, for physical treatment, and a chaplain for social, emotional, and spiritual support.

Although hospice can, and usually is, centered in the home, the patient may need to be admitted to a hospital, extended-care facility, or a hospice inpatient facility. The hospice personnel can arrange for inpatient care and will remain involved in the patient's treatment and with the patient's family; the patient can go back to in-home care as soon as possible.

At some point during hospice care, the patient's family and caregivers may need some time away from intense caregiving. Hospice service may offer them a break through respite care, which is often done in five-day periods. During this time the patient is cared for either in the hospice facility or in contracted beds in nursing homes or hospitals. Families can plan a mini-vacation, go to special events, or simply get much-needed rest at home while the patient is cared for in an inpatient setting.

Bereavement is another area where hospice shines. The hospice care team works with surviving family members to help them through the grieving process. A trained volunteer, clergy member, or professional counselor provides support to survivors through visits, phone calls, and/or written contact, as well as through support groups. The hospice team can refer family members and caregiving friends to other medical or professional care if needed. Bereavement services are often provided for about a year after the patient's death.

Hospice care is defined not only by the services and care provided, but also by the setting in which these services are delivered. Hospice care may be provided in your home or in a special facility. More than 90 percent of the hospice services provided in this country are based in patients' homes.

Many, if not all, of the home health agencies in your community, as well as independently owned hospice programs, will offer home hospice services. While a nurse, doctor, and other professionals serve as staff for the home hospice program, the key primary caregiver is usually a family member or friend who is responsible for around-the-clock supervision of the patient. This person is with the patient most of the time and is trained by the nurse to provide much of the hands-on care.

It is important to know that home hospice may require that someone be home with the patient at all times. This may be a problem if you live alone, or if your partner or adult children have full-time jobs. However, creative scheduling and good teamwork among your friends and loved ones can usually overcome this problem. Members of the hospice staff will visit regularly to check on you and your family and give needed care and services.

As I have said before, I had firsthand experience with hospice when my brother died in Oklahoma, and the hospice workers were just great. They were tremendously helpful and as efficient as a fine-tuned clock. I cannot praise them enough.

CHAPTER NINE
EUTHANASIA

We must recognize, even though we do not want to, that from the instant of conception in the womb, we all begin the journey through life which will eventually end in death. Therefore, these are the questions, among others, that can be raised: does "living" mean simply "existing?" Doesn't it mean, rather, the whole of life? Is it right that the aim of every doctor should be to conquer death? Shouldn't all of us, instead, try everything we can to ensure a person's capacity to live to the fullest extent of his or her abilities? Living isn't meant simply exhibiting one or two vital signs, such as respiration or the registration of a heartbeat. What is meant, rather, is the whole conglomeration of sensual experiences that a person calls "being alive"—the experiences that by their very complexity and subtlety are not amenable to measurement or statistical analysis and are usually known only to the patient, his closest associates, and perhaps his doctor.

Death is our only certainty. Why then should it not be seen as the natural and appropriate end to a complete and satisfying existence?

Today there are questions being raised by those who believe that to have dignity in death, it is not wrong to submit to euthanasia and/or suicide—and certainly they are questions that provide food for thought. Let me hasten to say that I do not, for the most part, believe in active euthanasia or suicide. I will, however, list reasons others have given in favor of it, so you can make up your own mind. However, I certainly do believe in passive euthanasia, which I will discuss later in this chapter.

Generally speaking, it is only the living that fear death, not the dying. Rather than worrying about when the moment of death comes (which is now defined in most cases as brain death), wouldn't it be more sensible to be worried and concerned about when "being alive" ceases? In this context, dying can be defined as the irreversible deterioration of the quality of life that precedes the death of a particular individual.

We must come to grips with the fact that death is not always the enemy; often it is good medical treatment that is the enemy. Often death achieves what medicine cannot always achieve—it stops suffering.

In terminal illness, the primary aim should no longer be to preserve life but to make the life that remains as comfortable and meaningful as possible. Thus, what may be appropriate treatment in an acutely ill patient, may be inappropriate for the dying patient.

Cardiac resuscitation, artificial respiration, intravenous infusions, nasogastric tubes, antibiotics—all are primary supportive measures for use in acute illnesses, to assist a patient through the initial period toward recovery and health. To use such measures in the terminally ill, with no expectancy of a return to health, is generally inappropriate and barbaric and is therefore bad medicine by definition.

It is, however, not a question of "to treat" or "not to treat," but what is appropriate treatment from a biological point of view, in light of the patient's personal and social circumstances.

"Euthanasia" comes from the Greek word meaning "an easy or painless death." There are two categories of euthanasia that have been discussed: active euthanasia and passive euthanasia.

Active euthanasia is when life is ended by direct intervention, such as giving a patient a lethal dose of a drug, or suicide.

Passive euthanasia is when death results from withdrawal or withholding of life-support systems or life-sustaining medications.

When the quality of life fails and there is an increase in suffering, should the doctor then attempt, with all the means at his disposal, to prolong the existence of the patient? The term "existence" is used because it is debatable whether the patient is really still alive. Or, from that time onward, should the doctor concentrate on improving the quality of dying, even if this may hasten the death of the patient?

It is such a very thin line. Is it wrong to let death and peace come? Or is it unethical to intervene at this point to allow the patient to see another day of suffering?

Most of us who insist that a doctor should not actually help a patient end the distress of dying are really not qualified to make that judgment. We are disqualified by reason of our noninvolvement. The relevant question is that of the dying patient, or the relatives who know what the patient's requirements are or have watched their loved one's prolonged suffering.

Those who claim that one can always alleviate the suffering of the dying have either not had enough exposure to the problem or are lacking in a simple quality—compassion.

Permit me to point out how incongruous our attitudes are toward death and dying. Society's attitude toward the different ways of causing the death of an individual is both hypocritical and illogical.

Consider that for as long as man has inhabited the earth, he has accepted, with very few reservations, the right to kill on the battlefield, even when this leads to not only his own death, but multiple deaths.

In this country, the demand for more liberal abortion laws has resulted in a human wave of abortions. Millions of lives are almost literally washed down the drain. But should the baby be born and the mother immediately chooses to flush it down the drain, then it is murder. And consider the hue and cry of horror by people when a doctor asks for the right to actively end the suffering of a terminally ill patient. Usually this is done when the patient is very old and has come to end of his life. But the abortion of a baby is when the person is just starting life . Where is the logic and reasoning?

Passive euthanasia is becoming more and more accepted by the medical profession, religious leaders, and society at large. Therefore, when it is permissible for treatment to be stopped or not instituted to allow the patient to die, it makes for small mercy and less sense when the next logical step—of actively terminating life and hence suffering—is not taken. Why, at this point, can't a life be brought to an end, instead of extending the suffering of the patient by hours, days, weeks, or even months?

Is not a deliberate act of omission, when death is the goal or purpose sought, morally indistinguishable from a deliberate act of commission? Procedurally, there is a difference between active and passive euthanasia, but the outcome is one and the same.

When discussing active euthanasia, the same questions are raised again and again: Who will decide when a life should be terminated, and how can mistakes be avoided? Would doctors perhaps misuse the right to take a life by getting rid of the people they do not like? Would the medical profession lose much of the respect and trust that is placed in them? Does the doctor have the right to play God? Shouldn't God be the arbiter on the taking of life?

It is feared by many that the doctor is playing God when he helps a patient to end his life. However, it can be just as readily argued that he is playing God when he keeps a person alive.

Generally, these same questions can be raised about war, capital punishment, and abortion. Many believe if doctors were given the right to practice active euthanasia, and all the necessary safeguards were developed, most of these objections would disappear. It is food for thought.

If it is playing God to reduce the time of suffering, then I guess many would believe that the God of mercy and compassion wouldn't mind if we mortals played God under such circumstances.

What do we know of God's interpretation of life? Is it the mere presence of a beating heart and respiratory functions, or is it something far more complex? I do not have any doubt that when God made man in his image and breathed life into him, he had a different concept of the meaning of life than the drug-saturated, pain-crazed patient, who may not eventually even feel the pain, but feels no contact with reality either, or the thrashing around on a sweat-soaked bed of a body whose mind is darkened in agony, its only reaction being the purely animal one of trying to escape pain.

I read a story once of a person who was admitted to the hospital at the age of seventy-eight years. His condition was described in his own words: "The engine is broken down and it is time for the engineer to abandon it."

Despite his request to leave him alone so he could die with dignity, medical treatment was instituted and increased until eventually he was intubated and connected to a mechanical respirator. The night he was connected to the respirator, he woke up, reached over and switched off the ventilator, and died. But before he lost consciousness he had time to scrawl a message to his physician. It read, "Death is not the enemy, doctor, inhumanity is!"

What role, then, can society play in preventing this kind of inhumanity that occurs every day in large hospitals, where patients are treated, not to alleviate their suffering, but often because some doctors want to try out their mastery of death-delaying techniques?

Society can ask for three things: that doctors be humanitarian and not merely scientists; that life-support systems and other aspects of modern medical technology not be used where there is no hope; and that when the patient is suffering from severe pain, that the pain be relieved by medicines, even if this means shortening the life of the patient. I have been present in far too many cases where the nurses will say, "We can't give him any more morphine, as he may become addicted." Really! What difference does it make, if he is dying?

This, I believe, is what is meant by passive euthanasia. It allows the medical staff to give the terminally ill patient a comfortable, dignified death. A doctor who holds such a viewpoint is not trying to kill his patients; rather he believes they have a right to die in comfort.

A word of caution when talking about life-sustaining apparatuses: in some states, if you have the patient put on life-sustaining respirators, for example, and then later "pull the plug," you can be accused of *active* euthanasia.

Generally, then, I believe the supreme value in our religious heritage is placed on the personhood of mankind, the person in his wholeness, his freedom, his integrity, and dignity. When illness brings a person to a state in which he is less than free, and less able to sustain his dignity and integrity, then what is most precious is gone.

The obvious conclusion, then, is that when personhood is gone, more continuation of existence by means of artificial life-support is a violation of an individual's right. What better argument is there in favor of society's acceptance of the use of passive euthanasia?

Question: I have always wondered at the kind of a person who would mercifully end the life of a suffering animal, yet would hesitate to extend the same privilege to a fellow human being. In short, why are we more merciful to our animals than we are to one another? This is certainly, I believe, food for thought and consideration.

CHAPTER TEN
TO THE FAMILY AND LOVED ONES OF THE DYNG PATIENT

In the following chapters I would like to speak to the family and loved ones of the dying patient. In this chapter I would like to cover what you should expect as the patient approaches death. In **Chapter Eleven** I will cover making plans for the funeral service. In **Chapter Twelve** I will cover grief and bereavement.

When a person enters the final stage of the dying process, several things take place. Physically the body begins the final process of shutting down. Usually this is an orderly and undramatic progression of physical changes, which are not medical emergencies. These changes are completely normal and are to be expected.

Then there is the emotional, spiritual, mental phase, which is a different kind of process completely. The spirit of the dying person begins the process of release from the body. This release tends to follow its own priorities, which may include the resolution of any unfinished business of a practical nature and the acceptance of permission to "let go" by the family members. These events are the normal, natural way in which the spirit prepares to move from this existence into the next dimension of life. The most appropriate kinds of responses to the emotional, spiritual, and mental changes are those that support and encourage this release and transition.

The experience we call death occurs when the body completes its natural process of shutting down and when the spirit completes its natural process of reconciling and finishing. Believe me, no matter how much you think you are prepared for the final breath of your loved one, you are not. I have been present in hundreds of cases where the patient has taken his or her final breath, and it is always a shock.

The emotional, spiritual, mental, and physical signs and symptoms of impending death are offered to help you understand the natural kinds of things that may happen and how you can respond appropriately. Of course not all of the signs and symptoms will occur with every person, nor will they occur in this order. Each person is different and needs to do things in his or her own way. This is not a time to change or try to influence your loved one, but the time to give full acceptance, support, and comfort.

The dying patient's hands and arms, feet, and then legs will be increasingly cool to the touch, and at the same time the color of the skin may change due to the blood being pooled around the major and vital organs of the body in order to protect them. In psychological terms this called the "fight or flight" response. Keep the person reasonably warm with a blanket, but remember the patient may not feel cold and may try to remove the blanket. If so, uncover him.

The patient will no doubt begin to sleep more and appear to be less communicative or unresponsive and at times be difficult to arouse. Sit with your loved one, hold his hand, but do not shake it, or him, to make him wake up. Speak to him in a soft voice, and remember, again, that the hearing is the last of the senses to be lost. Knowing that, do not speak about the person with someone else in the person's presence. You may be talking about what you are going to have for dinner, but the patient will "know" you are talking about him. Speak to the patient as you normally would, even if you do not get a response. *Never assume the patient is not hearing you.*

The patient may seem to be confused at times. He may not know the identity of people who are in the room or talking to him. Therefore, always identify yourself when talking with the patient, rather than asking the patient to guess who you are. Speak softly, clearly, and honestly when you need to communicate something important for the patient's comfort.

The patient may lose control of his urine or bowels as the muscles in those areas begin to relax. Try to use a rubberized sheet to protect the bed, and always try to keep your loved one clean and comfortable.

The patient may have gurgling sounds in his chest, sometimes called the "death rattle"; again, these changes are to be expected, due to decreased fluid intake and the inability to cough up the secretions that accumulate. Sometimes this can be eliminated or alleviated by turning the patient's head to the side and letting gravity take over. It is a good idea at this time to swab the mouth out with water or glycerin using a cotton swab. It is also advisable to swab the lips with Vaseline to keep them from getting chapped.

The patient may become quite restless and pick at the bedclothes or wave his arms in the air. This can be due to lack of oxygen in the brain. At this time it is good to speak softly to the person, stroke his forehead, or hold his hand, if possible. Do not try to stop him from what he is doing as that will only cause more unrest. Playing soothing music will often calm the person.

Almost always the person's appetite will diminish rapidly. He will not be hungry, and even the smell of food can bother him. Do not try to force the person to eat or drink; this only makes him much more uncomfortable and irritable. This may be an indication the person is ready for the final shutdown. Small chips of ice, like those put into a person's mouth after surgery, can be soothing. Sometimes a cool, damp cloth on the forehead is helpful. However, if the person seems to try to keep you from applying any of these apparent comforts, don't force it upon him. Sometimes, like in cancer and other diseases, even touch can be very painful to the patient. This is the time that you must observe the nonverbal communication. The person usually won't tell you outright to stop whatever it is that is bothering him, because he is afraid that will force you away from him; so he tries to let you know through nonverbal actions.

Breathing patterns will change as the person nears the end. Sometimes the patient will breathe very shallow breaths and even stop breathing altogether for several seconds and then take a deep breath and begin breathing regularly again. These are times when you will be sure he is gone, only to change your mind a few seconds later. Be aware of your emotions, as they will be on a virtual roller coaster during the final moments or sometimes even days. Sometimes you will get to the point where you wish the person would die and get it over with, and then you feel guilty for feeling that way. *These are all normal and natural feelings, so don't think something is wrong with you.*

At times the patient may begin talking to friends and members of his family who had died before. These are not necessarily hallucinations, and you should not try to contradict, argue, explain away, or belittle the patient, or tell him that is silly. Just because you cannot see or hear what's going on does not mean it is not real for the patient. Just affirm his or her experience.

The time will come when the patient will want only a certain significant person or persons with him as he travels the final road. If you are not in this select group, don't feel bad. It does not mean that you are loved less or not important. It more likely means that the patient has already said his goodbyes to you and is ready to make the transition. If you are in the inner circle at this time, be sure to give the patient your affirmation, support, and more than anything, your permission for him to die. At this time kiss, hug, cry, hold, or express whatever you most need to say, verbally and nonverbally.

Giving permission for your loved one to let go, without making him or her feel guilty for leaving, or trying to keep him or her with you to meet your own needs, can be very difficult. A dying person will normally try to hold on, even though it brings prolonged discomfort and even pain, in order to be sure that those who are going to be left behind will be all right. Therefore , your ability to release the dying person from this concern and give him or her assurance that it is all right to let go, whenever he or she is ready, is one of the greatest gifts you have to give your loved one at this time.

When the person is ready to die and you are able to let go, then it is time for you to say good-bye. Saying good-bye is your final gift of love to your loved one. It may be as simple as saying, "I love you!" It may include recounting favorite memories, places to which you have traveled, activities you shared. It may include saying you are sorry for whatever things that made strife in your lives. Or you may recount the things for which you are thankful. Whatever it is, let it all hang out—you will feel better for it. Tears are normal, God gave them to you for occasions like this. They do not need to be hidden from your loved one, or apologized for. Tears express your love and will help you to let go.

How will you know when death has occurred? The signs of death include such things as no breathing, no heartbeat, release of bowel or bladder, no response, eyelids slightly open, pupils enlarged, eyes fixed on a certain spot, no blinking, jaw relaxed, and mouth slightly open.

Remember, the body does not have to be removed immediately. Wait until you are ready. If you or your family want to assist in preparing the body by bathing or dressing it, that may be done. Don't call the funeral home until you are sure you are ready to have the body removed. Take your time with your loved one, as this will be the last time you will have that opportunity, until you meet again in the hereafter.

CHAPTER ELEVEN
THE FUNERAL SERVICE

Your loved one has died, and now comes perhaps the hardest thing you have ever done: prepare for the final rites and disposition of the body. First, I will make a list of the important things that must be done almost immediately after the patient dies, many of which can be planned for and carried out when a person first approaches the task of putting his affairs in order, and long before the need arises. At the end of this chapter I will include a checklist of the things that need to be taken care of immediately. Secondly, I will discuss the last rites and why they are important.

When you are notified that your love one has died, or if she has died at home, you will be dazed and grief-stricken, and you will want to just be by yourself and left alone. However, there are some tasks that have to be taken care of right away and will not wait. In a very real sense this is a blessing, as it keeps your mind active and protects you from the harshness of the death, if only for a little while. These tasks include the following:

- Ascertain fact of death. Call your doctor, coroner, and/or police in case of sudden death.
- If body parts are to be donated, be sure your doctor knows.
- Call a mortuary or funeral home for removal of the body. (If a person dies in a hospital or nursing home, these organizations are required by law, in some states, for immediate removal of the body.)
- Notify your minister, rabbi, or another religious leader.
- Notify the memorial society if your loved one has so specified.
- Notify a trusted friend or friends to come and be with you for emotional support and help.
- Notify relatives and other business associates.

- Notify your lawyer, if you have one. (His advice may be essential in dealing with bank accounts, will, probate, etc.)
- Immediately remove items from the bank safety deposit box, jointly held by you and your deceased spouse , because as soon as an obituary is listed in the newspaper, the bank officials are required by law in some states to put a seal on the box, and you may not be allowed access to it for several weeks.
- Check the deceased's papers for funeral plans or preferences. Also check with the deceased's church to see if any plans are on file.

The above-mentioned are the essential things that must be done right away. Next you should consult with your clergyperson to make arrangements for funeral or memorial service. Check for his availability at both the service and interment. Discuss the type of service you would like to have, whether to be held in the church or the funeral home, make suggestions for its content (poetry, scripture, biographical material), and indicate musical preferences, whether instrumental or vocal, and hymns or other selections to be included.

Consult with the funeral director. Discuss with him what is to be done with the remains. There are three possibilities: cremation, burial, or donation of the body to a medical school. (Bear in mind that medical schools frequently have more bodies than they need, and if the medical school is out of state, shipping charges can be very high and must be paid by the family.)

Be aware that embalming may not be necessary, particularly if you are opting for cremation. Also bear in mind that funerals can be very expensive, and the funeral home, out of necessity, must charge for everything they do: print folders, arrange flowers, come to the church to pass out folders, supply limousines, arrange for thank-you cards, and so on.

Determine the place of interment: grave site, or crypt for ashes. Many churches now have a columbarium, which usually costs much less than cemetery plots. Some cemeteries also require a vault if the person is to be buried. If the deceased was a veteran, he or she may be buried, or put in a crypt, in a veterans' cemetery free of charge, including a headstone or crypt plaque. This also includes a space for the spouse.

Provide the funeral director with the necessary information (see the accompanying form below). Provide burial clothing, which does not have to be new but may be something especially liked by the deceased. If the service is to be held in the funeral parlor, be sure the time matches the availability of the clergyperson. Personally, I always tried my best to be available, no matter what time of day or night, but sometimes it is impossible. Many times the clergyperson is the last one to be notified, and he or she may not always be available.

If your loved one belonged to lodges or fraternal organizations, consult with them if their type of service is desired.

Make a choice of cemetery. Your funeral director can help in this matter. While an arrangement for grave opening is made by the funeral director, the lot must be chosen and purchased by the family. The sexton will show available space and will make out the deed and collect payment for the lot either in one lump sum or by contract, depending upon the policy of the cemetery. Cemeteries often impose a higher charge for lots bought at the time of need. Remember, a lot of states, like Arizona, allow scattering of ashes wherever a person wishes.

I am a lover of mountains, so I wouldn't mind my ashes being scattered among the mountaintops. I am also a veteran, so interment is available for me in the national veterans' cemetery.

When arranging your own affairs, keep in mind that the loved ones you leave behind have to live with the decisions you make, so don't cast your wishes "in concrete ;" —you are not the one who has to live with them. With all of the above details that have to be considered, I am sure you now see the importance of talking these things over with family members and have your wishes written down, well in advance, before any of these steps have to be taken. It is very important, at any age, to have your affairs in order.

For the bereaved, friends can be a tremendous help at this time. Let them answer telephone calls, or make calls to relatives and friends. Let them take over the kitchen, serving meals, coffee, or snacks, as well as keeping a list of things brought in by others. Let them help by providing transportation for errands, picking up people at the airport, or by driving your family car. Another big help would be to have others arrange sleeping accommodations for relatives and friends of the deceased from out of town. Don't think that you are imposing on your friends and relatives—they will be glad to help.

By all means avoid making hasty decisions. I have always told the loved ones of the deceased not to make any major decisions for at least a year. Almost always, a snap decision turns out to be the wrong decision. Weighty decisions will be more carefully made after the initial shock is dissipated and the slow wisdom of grief has brought its healing.

A case in point: One woman I told this to didn't heed my advice. She sold her home shortly after the memorial service and moved to live in the same town as her children in another state. She soon found out that her children had their own circle of friends and things to do and didn't have nearly as much time to spend with her as she had hoped. She came back and told me how sorry she was and that she should have listened to me. In fact, she bought another home and stayed in the area where her longtime friends lived, rather than go back to where her kids lived.

You should consult your banker, as he may make suggestions that will help you arrange your financial matters wisely.

Also consult your insurance representative. He will help you with the problems you may face in securing settlements with your insurance companies. It will be a big help to him if you have a list of your policies, their location, the companies that are involved, and the amounts.

Your funeral home will get additional copies of the death certificate for a fee. You will need quite a few copies, as the following people or organizations will need them: your bank; your insurance companies; your lawyer; the Social Security Administration, the Veterans Administration, and more. It may be a good idea to check with a trusted friend who has gone through this ordeal to get an idea of how many copies you will need.

Though it will be very difficult and emotionally draining, this would probably be a good time to sort out and dispose of your loved one's clothing and personal effects, while your relatives and friends are around to help you and give emotional support. This can be devastating to do if you are all by yourself.

The Funeral Service

The funeral service or memorial service is extremely important as it gives all of the family, relatives, friends and acquaintances the opportunity to come and say goodbye to their loved one or friend, give support to the family, and offer them a chance to begin the grieving process. This is a tremendous comfort to the survivors. Having a time of refreshment and conversation following the service is also a good opportunity to offer one's condolences to the survivors and share what the deceased meant to them.

The family of the deceased should be encouraged to have a service of celebration rather than a service of mourning - a service celebrating the life of the deceased rather than a service mourning the passing of their loved one. I would always meet the family a day or two before the actual service and ask them to "free-associate" about their loved one. In other words, let them talk about the deceased and what he or she meant to them. While they talked I would write down things they said. Then I would take all of these ramblings back to my office and write the service homily. I always tried to make the service very personal and upbeat.

Many times after the service people would say to me, "You must have known him all your life, you knew so much about him." The fact is I may have never known the person before doing his service. This happened many times while serving a church in Maine. There they seemed to come in out of the woods.

I was always known for my funeral services in every church that I served. In fact, I have been asked by many Catholic friends to do their service, or the service of their loved one, because, they said, "You make them so personal, loving, warm and compassionate." The funeral service is one of the most important services a pastor can offer to his or her parishioners. It is a time for the most intimate of relationships and a great opportunity to be of so much help and support.

The family should be encouraged to view the body of their loved one before the funeral service or the cremation. The reason for this is an attempt to make the death "real" to them. If they view the body there is no way they can deny that a death has taken place.

My older brother died in California while I was leading a group to Alaska. He was immediately cremated but they held off having the service until we returned so my wife and I could attend. By not seeing the body it was difficult for me to come to grips with his death. I kept thinking he was away on a trip or something. Intellectually, of course, I knew he had died, but emotionally it was hard for me to accept. Be aware of how easy it is to deceive ourselves.

The minister should always discourage an open casket during the service, or opening the casket after the service. The minister, in the service, does his best to help the people accept the death of their loved one and move on to the grief stage. Having the casket open during the service, or opening it after the service, opens the wound all over again and the minister's words are forgotten.

Checklist for Things to Be Done Immediately Following Death

- ❏ Call funeral home.
- ❏ Decide on time and place of funeral or memorial service.
- ❏ Prepare copy for printed notice.
- ❏ Make list of immediate family, close friends, employer, business colleagues, and notify by phone.
- ❏ If flowers are to be omitted, decide on an appropriate memorial to which gifts may be given.
- ❏ Write obituary: include age, place of birth, cause of death, occupation, college degrees, memberships held, military service, outstanding accomplishments, list of survivors in immediate family; give time and place of funeral or memorial service. Deliver the obituary in person or phone newspapers. Funeral directors usually take care of this after you have written it.
- ❏ Notify insurance companies, including automobile, life, health, for immediate cancellation and available refund.
- ❏ Arrange for members of family or friends to take turns answering the doorbell and/or phone, keeping careful records of calls.
- ❏ Arrange hospitality for visiting relatives and friends.
- ❏ Arrange appropriate child care.
- ❏ Coordinate supplying of food for the next few days. If food is brought in, have a designated person keep close record of who brought what and in what kind of container if it needs to be returned.

❑ Consider special needs of the household as for cleaning, cooking, straightening up, etc., which could be done by friends.

❑ Select special pallbearers and notify them by phone. (If a casket is involved, make sure the people you select are able to carry it. Do not select people with heart problems, back problems, etc. You could make them honorary pallbearers.)

❑ Notify lawyer and executor.

❑ Get several copies of death certificate.

❑ Plan for disposition of flowers after funeral (take home, give to nursing homes, hospitals, etc.)

❑ Prepare list of distant persons to be notified by letter and/or printed service bulletins.

❑ Prepare list of persons to receive acknowledgment for flowers, cards, food, calls, donations, etc., and send appropriate notes of thanks.

❑ Check carefully all life and casualty insurance and death benefits, including Social Security, pensions, military, credit unions, trade unions, fraternity, etc. Check also on income for survivors from these sources.

❑ Check promptly on all debts and installment payments. Some carry insurance clauses that will cancel them. If there is any delay meeting some obligations, consult with creditors and ask for more time *before* the payments are due.

❑ If the deceased was living alone, notify landlord and utilities. Also notify post office where to forward mail.

❑ TAKE PRECAUTIONS AGAINST THIEVES AND SCAMS. NOTIFY POLICE TO WATCH YOUR HOME DURING FUNERAL OR MEMORIAL SERVICE.

Form - G

FOR THE GUIDANCE OF MY SURVIVORS

Basic Information for Death Certificate and Obituary Notices

Name:	(last)	(first)	(middle)
Address:	(number and street)		
	(city)	(state)	(zip code)
Single ☐	**Married** ☐	**Widowed** ☐	**Divorced** ☐
Date of Birth:	(day)	(month)	(year)
Place of Birth:	(city) (county)	(state)	(country)
Location of Birth Certificate:			
Social Security Number:			
Veteran (if you were not a veteran, leave this section blank)			
(name of war) (branch of service)	(unit)		(rank)
Commendations / Medals:			
Employment **Retired?** Yes ☐ No ☐	(if retired, indicate previous employment)		
Primary Occupation:			
Employer:			
City:	**State:**		
Father's Name:	(last)	(first)	(middle)
Mother's Name:	(last)	(first)	(middle)
Name of Spouse or Immediate Relative:	(last/maiden)	(first)	(middle)
Address of Spouse or Immediate Relative:	(city)	(state)	(zip)
Telephone Number:	**Cell Phone Number:**		

Form - H

FOR THE GUIDANCE OF MY SURVIVORS, cont.

Other Close Relatives

Name	City	State	Relationship	Phone Number

Your Church Membership

(name of church)　　　　　　(address)　　　　　　(phone number)

Offices Held or Participation:

Major Lifetime Achievements / Other Personal Information

Scholastic (include schools diplomas, degrees, honor societies, fraternities, etc.):

Athletic:

Professional (include jobs held, awards, etc.):

Fraternal Organizations (include office held):

Social Organizations (include office held):

Community Organizations (include office held):

Hobbies and Interests:

Other:

Form - I

Funeral Arrangements (choose A, B, or C)

A. Gift of Life Program		
Is the body to be delivered to hospital for organ transplant or medical use? Yes ☐ No ☐		
Hospital:	Phone:	
Physician:	Phone:	
B. Burial Procedure		
1. Is body to be embalmed? Yes ☐ No ☐		
2. Suggested funeral home:	Phone:	
3. Type of casket desired (i.e., wood or steel):		
4. Suggested price limit:		
5. Name of preferred cemetery:	Lot #:	
6. Funeral is to be: Public ☐ Private ☐		
7. Location of visitation:		
Is casket to be present? Yes ☐ No ☐ Open ☐ Closed ☐		
8. Location of funeral service:		
9. Graveside service? Yes ☐ No ☐		
10. Suggested Pallbearers:		
a.	Phone:	
b.	Phone:	
c.	Phone:	
d.	Phone:	
e.	Phone:	
f.	Phone:	
11. Honorary Pallbearers:		
a.	Phone:	
b.	Phone:	
c.	Phone:	
d.	Phone:	
12. Additional Instructions:		

Form - J

Funeral Arrangements, cont.

C. Cremation Procedures
1. Suggested funeral home: Phone:
2. Disposition of remains
a. Burial - site & lot number:
b. Scattered - preferred site:
c. Columbarium - location:
d. Other:
3. Memorial service to be: Public ☐ Private ☐
4. Preferred location of memorial service:
5. Additional instructions:

D. Arrangements for Funeral or Memorial Service
1. Suggestions for sacred or secular literature:
a.
b.
c.
2. Suggested music:
a.
b.
c.
3. Suggested speaker(s):
a.
b.
c.
4. Additional instructions:
5. Flowers acceptable? Yes ☐ No ☐
6. Memorial causes:
7. Other requests or instructions:

Form - K

Signature Page

All the attached forms have been completed by me, at my own initiative, for the guidance of my survivors at the time of my death. Unless otherwise specified, I have listed preferences which may be changed or altered at the discretion of my survivors.

Signature:_____

Date:_____

Copies of these forms should be sent to the following people:

1.
2.
3.
4.
5.
6.

The original of these forms should be kept with your important papers or trust folder.
Do not put it in your bank safety deposit box.

CHAPTER TWELVE
MOURNING, GRIEF, AND BEREAVEMENT

I am an avid reader of the comic strip *Peanuts* by Charles Schulz. But there is one statement that is included quite often and always bothers me: "Good grief, Charlie Brown!" I don't know about you, but I do not see anything in "grief" that is "good." They just do not go together; they seem to be a contradiction in terms, or total opposites. Can "grief" ever be "good"?

Have you ever experienced the following: "I am tired and exhausted all the time. I can hardly move. My stomach is terribly upset—it seems to get better for a while, and then I feel terrible again. I have a feeling of tightness in my throat. I choke and can't seem to catch my breath. I seem to have to sigh all the time. I have an empty feeling in my abdomen. I feel tense—as if my brain actually hurts. I don't want anyone to come near me. I am afraid if they ask me what is wrong, or how I feel, I will break right down and cry, and I certainly don't want to do that. Please stay away from me and leave me alone."

Chances are that most of you have felt like this before. It may have been when you lost a loved one; or when you encountered severe marital problems; or when you lost your job; or when you were threatened with a divorce, or were in fact separated or divorced; or when you lost a beloved pet, etc.

This, my friends, is "grief"—or, to be technical, it is the "grief syndrome." But it still boils down to plain, ordinary grief. If you have not experienced it, you most certainly will sooner or later. I am sure that those of you who are reading this book have experienced it or are contemplating experiencing it. Now, can these feelings in any way, shape, or form be called "good"?

Experts in the field of grief have come up with ten stages of the grieving process. I have witnessed these ten stages, but every person does not go through all of them, and it is quite common for a person to go through a few of the stages and then go back to square one and start all over again. Or he may bounce back and forth from the first stage to the last, or the third to the fifth, or the last back to the first, and so on.

Now, grieving is also felt by the dying person who is facing his last days on earth. I have also witnessed "pre-grief" by the loved ones surrounding the dying person. They sometimes go through the whole process before the person dies. Sometimes this is enough, but other times they will go right back through all the stages again. The stages are

1. **Shock:** Almost all people will go through this stage first. This happens when a person first learns he has a terminal illness, as well as when the loved ones find out a person has died. In many ways this is a helpful stage, because it seems to anesthetize the survivors against the overwhelming loss. They do not comprehend, and are not able to face the full magnitude of it.

2. **Emotional release:** This is the beginning of realizing how dreadful the loss is. Venting and releasing these feelings is much better than trying to repress them. People need to grieve. They need to get these feelings outside themselves. Therefore, they need listeners. The listeners must be those who can provide a caring presence. It has nothing to do with saying the right things, as though any of us, including clergy, could say the "right" thing that would make a difference. In the first place, the grieving person hardly ever can recall what a person says to them, but he can almost always recall that you were there to listen to how he felt and thought. He will also recall the hugs and hand holding and touches that you administered during his time of need.

3. **Depression, loneliness, and utter isolation:** The person sinks into the depths of despair. He feels that there is no help for him. He should be assured that this is a normal feeling. However, because this is a dangerous stage, and suicide is often the first thought going through the person's mind, there should be a lot of concern expressed by those around the grieving person. There is a human need to grieve and not pass by this inevitability too quickly, to be too quickly assured that if, for example, he had faith he would not grieve, or that it is unmanly for men to shed tears. There has been more psychological damage done to men by hearing advice like "Big boys don't cry" than any other thing of which I know. Big boys do, and definitely should, cry for their own emotional well-being. Our grief must take place when the death occurs, lest later on it reasserts itself in some pathological form (this is called morbid grief, which I will cover later in this chapter).

4. **Physical symptoms of distress:** Many times the stress of handling the death of a loved one causes real physical ailments. I can't count how many times the spouse, or some other loved one, of a person who has died lands

in a hospital very soon after the funeral. Stress definitely does take its toll. The best recourse is to seek out a person who understands the grief process to whom you can talk, and who will let you vent your feelings.

5. **Panic:** The person who is convinced "something is wrong with me as a person" can concentrate on little else. He may fear he is losing his mind. The best help is to make clear that his feelings are normal and that others are feeling the same way.

6. **Guilt feelings:** Out of the hundreds of people I have helped through the grieving process, I have never seen a person who does not feel guilt. I have heard many people say, "If only I had told him I loved him one more time." "If only I had kissed him before he left for work." "If only I had told her what a wonderful wife she was." "If only . . ." And on and on it goes. Many will recall past neglect or mistreatment—either physical or mental—toward the deceased. Wrongs may indeed be imaginary or blown out of proportion, but they are very real to the bereaved. They may also be real wrongs, with well-founded guilt. Many times I have helped people with their guilt by placing a chair in front of them and telling them, "The deceased (person's name) is sitting in that chair in front of you. Now tell him what you would like to say to him at this time." Confession and unburdening of real guilt often gives the person relief. Forgiveness of real wrongs as if they were imaginary is no adequate solution. Being human, we of course are imperfect, living in an imperfect world. We fail to do what we had planned to. We are continually letting things go by. We go on believing that there is always tomorrow. So tomorrow we will say the right thing, and do the right thing. We will carry out what has to be done. But when death occurs, there is that finality. There is no tomorrow. Thus the inevitability of guilt. "If only we hadn't said thus and so." "If only we had acted in time." "If only we had anticipated." "If only we had carried out what we had planned." The list goes on *ad infinitum.*

7. **Hostility:** Feeling worse leads to expressing oneself more actively. Hostile expressions toward those who "caused" the loss, either real or imaginary, are very common. Such feelings are real, but they should not be encouraged. Maybe the grieving person is angry at life, angry at the injustice that his loved one had to suffer like that. Maybe he is angry at the deceased because he or she left him. Maybe he should shake his fist in the face of God and ask why God made such an unjust world. When a person shares such feelings with me, I usually say, "Go ahead and rail at God; He has big shoulders and can take it." At the same time, however, the angry person might also be told that Jesus said "The rain falls on the just and the unjust." And God never promised us a rose garden. I remember visiting a Christian

woman who was dying of cancer, and I said, "Bev, why you? You have lived such a clean, wholesome Christian life and helped so many people. Why you?" She looked up at me and said, "Pastor, why not me? And besides, I will be spending Christmas with my Lord, and that is more than you can say." What a wonderful expression of faith and belief. I went to cheer her up, and instead she cheered me up.

8. **Inability to renew normal activities:** Not being able to go back to "business as usual" is a common complaint. The bereaved feels she must bear the loss alone, since others are back to normal activities. When she feels like this, she needs encouragement to face new realities, not to be sheltered from them. Many doctors will prescribe tranquilizers to the bereaved after the loss of a loved one. I believe this to be a mistake. It is much better to face the inevitable head-on rather than to postpone it. I have found that postponing will only increase the devastation as time goes by, and when she finally has to face the fact that her loved one is gone, it will be far more traumatic.

9. **Gradually overcoming the grief:** Emotional balance returns little by little, like the healing of a physical wound. Of course the rate varies with each individual. In my work with grieving people, I find it sometimes takes as much as a year to come back to reality. I get furious with people who will say; for example, "His wife is still grieving after two weeks, you would think she would be over it by now . . . ." In the first place, no one ever stops grieving, and if they do, it is not normal. To be sure, it gets easier as time goes by, but I will still get tears in my eyes when I think of our daughter whom we lost over fifty years ago. Believe me, there is no such thing as the hackneyed phrase "closure."

10. **Readjustment to new realities, or put another way, acceptance of what has happened:** This does not mean in any way that the bereaved will be his own self again, because he now has to face a new situation; but he may well be stronger, deeper, and even better for having faced and overcome this disaster in his life. How does he do this? He must set new goals for himself when he has lost a person so close to him. He must not dwell on where he is emotionally. He must look ahead. First of all, he must have emancipation from the dead. Some find this very difficult to do, and if they can't, it can lead to morbid grief. It is well known that not only the person dies at the time of his or her death. If a loved one cannot cope with what has happened, he or she, though still breathing, will also die, in a way. Sometime he will set an extra plate at the table and talk to an empty chair. Perhaps he turns her room into a shrine, keeping everything from yesteryear, and goes in and communes with her departed spirit. Perhaps he asks her what she wants him to do about this or that. What would she think about the best way

to handle things? What would she recommend? There are even those who take up a pseudo form of religion called spiritualism. They go to séances regularly so they can commune with the dead. But in order to begin living again, they must emancipate themselves from the dead. This must be their first and foremost goal. To be sure, this may take a long time to accomplish. The second goal is to establish a lifestyle based on being single again. Many times couples do not understand what they do to their friends who are newly widowed. They drift away. Not maliciously, nor intentionally, just inevitably. The single person must accommodate himself to living in the world of singles and establish a lifestyle accordingly. The third and final goal is the need to establish new friendships, because the friendships of the past, which are often based on a couples' world, will no longer work. New friends have to be made—different friends. Life has to be built on that reality. A good way to do this is join a singles club at a church. Everyone there is in the same boat.

In summation of this chapter, I would like to say that in any type of crisis, whether it is death or anything that creates a shock to the system, we will become sick or well based solely upon our capacity first to face up to it and not run from it, and secondly to accept it. There is no use feeling sorry for ourselves and endlessly blaming God, or life. This is just the way it is. I am well aware that it is easier said than done, but if after a year's time you still find yourself in deep grief and doing any of the above-mentioned abnormal things, I would strongly recommend that you seek grief counseling. I have done a lot of it, and believe me, it works. Do not feel that you are all alone in your struggle and have to work it out by yourself. Many people have taken this journey before you, and have made it through all right. Like coping with depression, most of the time you will not be able to accomplish this alone. Don't feel that something is wrong with you if you "break down" years after the death. Some aromas, views, conversations will take you back to the years you were together, and it will cause all the feelings to emerge. This is to be expected and is totally normal. By all means, do not think it is a sign of weakness to seek help; on the contrary, it is a sign of strength.

AUTHOR'S NOTE

In this book I have tried to cover all bases on getting your affairs in order but, of course, I am well aware of my human frailties and know that readers can come up with many things that I did not cover. I would welcome your comments and additions. In case the book goes to future printings, I would then be able to elaborate on some subjects, or even include new ones. You may get in touch by contacting me at education4living@cableone.net.

All the forms found in this book have been reproduced on a compact disc as forms that you can fill in on your computer and are downloadable from my web site: *Education4Living.com* or you can obtain a CD by contacting me. This will enable you to make copies for your family, relatives, doctors, hospitals, lawyers, and any others you think should know your wishes, without tearing those pages out of the book.

When I graduated from seminary I made a vow that I would spend the rest of my life helping people help themselves. God willing, I will be able to do that for many years to come.

It has been a pleasure for me to share with you, and I thank you for purchasing this book. My prayer is that it will help you along the way.

To order extra copies of this book, please contact me at the above e-mail address or via my home address:

Education 4 Living
P.O. Box 10271
Prescott, AZ 86304

About the Author

Gene W. Laramy answered the call to the Christian ministry later in life. He graduated from the University of Maine and the Bangor Theological Seminary in the same year and went on to earn his doctoral degree at the San Francisco Theological School. He furthered his studies at the Dr. Elisabeth Kübler-Ross Institute and the Menninger Foundation, as well as through many workshops. Dr. Laramy has served churches in Maine, Minnesota, Nebraska, and Arizona. He has conducted workshops throughout the United States on death, dying, and bereavement and on stress management using biofeedback. He is the author of the book, *What Do You Say, After You Say You're Sorry* (Vantage Press, 1985). He is founder and director of Education 4 Living, an organization with the purpose of helping people help themselves through education. He and his wife, Inez, have led educational tours for Nawas International Travel for thirty-seven years, traveling to many points of the globe. They have three sons, four grandchildren, and three great-grandchildren. Dr. Laramy is semiretired and lives with his wife in Prescott, Arizona. They recently celebrated their sixtieth wedding anniversary.